Toasters
and Small Kitchen Appliances

A PRICE GUIDE

© 1995

L-W BOOK SALES
P.O. Box 69
Gas City, IN 46933

ISBN#: 0-89538-039-0

Published by: L-W BOOK SALES
P.O. Box 69
Gas City, IN 46933

Please write for our free catalog.

Printed by IMAGE GRAPHICS, INC., Paducah, Kentucky

Table of Contents

Introduction

A tremendous period of growth occurred in North America following the Industrial Revolution. Once the American people weathered through the Great Depression, this era of economic well-being returned full-force, ensuring pride and financial stability once again for families throughout the states. The impact this Renaissance had upon family life was incredible. Homemakers and housewives everywhere had access to new technology which enabled their daily chores to proceed much swifter and easier. This new age of convenience led millions of families to encourage companies to fill the demand for all sorts of *electric appliances*.

Opportunists in the art of cooking and baking found many shiny new devices in their local department stores, brought them home and nestled them on the kitchen counter. Toasters, hot plates, coffee brewers, mixers, grills, popcorn poppers, waffle irons, and many other ingenious contraptions made a heartfelt contribution to the overworked pleas of a toiler in the home.

A multitude of manufacturers began the competition for shelf space which would last for decades. Some companies would grow and flourish, while others might begin strong yet later fall into obscurity. Designs of appliances would change and adapt as fast as customers would acquire them, usually at an alarming rate. The status quo at the time was leading to the American dream of an "all-electric kitchen". No longer just an aid to mealtime tasks, appliances would gather in a magnificent chrome array like brave soldiers clad in silver armor defending the woman's work area. Husbands eager to please the Mrs. wouldn't hesitate to bring a gleaming new instrument home during an anniversary or similar occasion (men already understood the insatiable appetite for tools of all sorts).

The leaders of the "appliance movement" built huge empires during this fortuitous season of capitalism, many of which still remain today. Westinghouse and General Electric continued to tighten their grasp on the market, yet still hundreds of competitors helped fill the demands of eager families. Monarch, Hotpoint, Sunbeam, Robeson Rochester Corp., Universal, and Manning-Bowman & Co. were but a handful of representatives during this marketing frenzy. Most of the companies involved produced quality merchandise which persuaded continued sales, while a few shortsighted producers filled orders with shabby equipment- much to the chagrin of the unfortunate consumer.

Due to its impact on the American lifestyle, the realm of electric appliances has lured a massive crowd of collectors. The fascinating combination of the "space age" and the "industrial age" provided a wealth of treasures throughout the 40's and 50's, and are surfacing daily as we know it. Opportunities to discover new additions to an appliance collection can be found fairly easily, if compared to other collectible fields which are also hot at the time. While antique dealers and collectors' malls may have already erected displays of appliances, garage sales, flea markets, and pawn shops also may be hiding a trove of enviable items. Appliances haven't yet garnered the high-cost reputation of other collectibles related to this era, and this is very fortunate to collectors at this time (however, remember they were kitchen appliances - they cost a pretty penny when brand new). If you include enthusiastic ambition along with your search, not only will your efforts bear fruit - it can be fun.

Acknowledgments

We would like to thank the following people who donated their appliances, reference materials, and or pictures, so that we could compile this price guide for you the collectors. Thanks to Gwen Goldman, Wayne Stoops and Phil Brandt for all of their help.

Pricing Note

The current values in this book should be used only as a guide. They are not intended to set prices, which vary from one section of the country to another. Auction prices as well as dealer prices vary greatly and are affected by condition as well as demand. The publisher nor the contributors assume responsibility for any losses or gains that might be incurred as a result of consulting this guide.

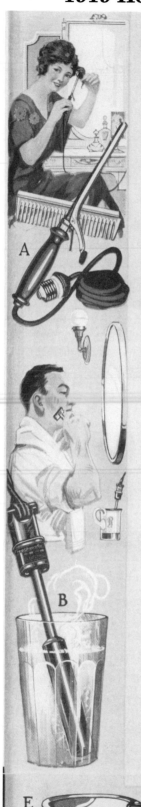

Hotpoint

How many servants await your bidding day and night always eager to serve?

For the answer, count the lamp sockets in your home.

Perhaps you use current only at Mazda-time, and allow your wiring system to lie idle most of the time.

So we suggest that you supply these eager servants with proper tools for their idle hours—

— use electricity to supplement your regular heat
— let it furnish hot water for shaving, baby's milk, etc.
— it is the ideal way to apply heat to the body
— in countless other ways it will serve you instantly

The comfort of your family will be immeasurably increased as you make greater use of electricity.

A All of the earlier methods of heating curling tongs are obsolete wherever electricity is available because this Hotpoint Curling Iron does away with the usual trouble and annoyances.

The electrically heated comb furnishes an ideal hair dryer.

B Plunged into water or any liquid Hotpoint Immersion Heater begins to heat immediately. It is therefore invaluable for heating small quantities of water for many purposes which suggest themselves.

The small size here shown is 7 inches long. Larger size for heavier duty. Crookneck to lie flat on the bottom of the dish.

E This Radiant Grill enables you to carry on two cooking operations at the same time, one above the glowing coils and the other below. Boils, broils, fries, toasts and by using Ovenette you secure a small but very efficient oven.

Three Heat Grill is furnished with dishes as illustrated. Ovenette is a separate appliance.

F More Hotpoint Irons have been sold than any other household electrical appliance, which is a fair measure of their value. Numerous special features, including the thumb rest; the attached stand; the hot point; cool handle; hinged plug.

3 lb. for dainty work, 5 or 6 lb. for household ironing.

C The instant the connection is made the wires glow cherry red and the Radiant Heater is a scintillating bowl of heat. "Warms as the Sun Warms." Attaches to any lamp socket. Uses about the same current as an electric iron.

Outside nickel and black enamel. Reflector of polished copper.

D The Hotpoint Safety Comfo is made of metal, sufficiently flexible to conform to the body curves. The heat can be maintained indefinitely under instant control of the user, even under the bedding, by moving a little switch as illustrated in the circle.

Extra long cord with separable plug conveniently located; sanitary eiderdown cover.

G The crunchiness of toast, delectably brown and hot from the Hotpoint Toaster adds new breakfast joy. So quick and convenient, too.

The detachable rack is an added convenience.

H Half a minute after you put the coffee and cold water into the percolator, the water begins to drip thru the coffee and in a few minutes is ready to pour—amber clear and piping hot.

Automatic safety switch prevents burn-outs and can be reset by anyone.

The pot illustrated is six-cup paneled style. There are several other styles in pots and urns at varying prices.

Ask your Hotpoint Dealer to Demonstrate

There are more than 10,000 places throughout the country where Hotpoint Appliances are on sale—Lighting Companies, Electrical Dealers, Hardware Dealers, Housefurnishing Stores, etc. Any of these Dealers will gladly demonstrate Hotpoint Appliances.

Edison Electric Appliance Company, Inc.
Chicago

New York   Ontario, Calif.   Atlanta

Manufacturers of the three well-known lines of electrical household appliances
Hotpoint   Edison   Hughes

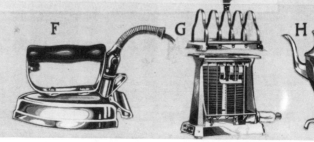

MODERN GIFTS THAT LAST FOR YEARS

Automatic Hotpoint "Florentine" Urn Set

A charming coffee set of matchless grace in form and ornament. Picture the joy when *this* gift is unwrapped! Its beauty will be preserved by gleaming Hotpoint Chromeplate—the life-time finish—and its long years of use safeguarded by its CALROD element and Super-Automatic Thermal Protector. Makes 9 cups of wonderful Hotpoint HOT-drip coffee. In Chromeplate, $48.00. Nickel finish, $38.50.

There are *many* models of Hotpoint percolators and sets from which you can choose. Prices from $8.45 to $65.00. All make most delicious, full-flavored, fragrant coffee by the exclusive HOT-drip method.

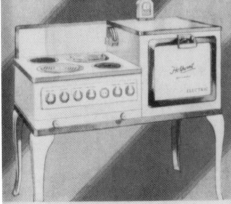

What Mother Really Wants
A Hotpoint *Automatic* Electric Range
"The Electric Maid for Modern Mothers"

Here's the great gift of gifts for wife or mother—for your *own* home. This *modern* Hotpoint automatic electric range. It will bake or roast for her *scientifically*, better than she ever thought possible, without the slightest attention on her part. She is *free* from the kitchen while the meals are cooking. And think of ootless cooking utensils, never to need scouring! Just pure, lean, *fast* heat at the turn of a switch. This is the fastest, most economical electric range ever made. Finished in white porcelain namel with gray trim and untarnishing Hotpoint Chromeplate. Equipped with the Hotpoint Thrift Cooker, HI-SPEED CALROD unit, automatic temperature control and patented Smokeless Broiler. The new combination clock and automatic imer may be added at a small extra cost. Ask your electric company for full information and their special Christmas offer.

HERE are gifts to delight the modern woman's heart. She'll take pride in their beauty . . . and joy in the daily convenience they afford.

These lovely gifts will keep fresh the memory of your thoughtfulness and affection every day for years to come. For these modern electrical gifts bear the treasured name "Hotpoint," assurance of enduring beauty and faithful service.

Only a few Hotpoint gift suggestions are shown here. Your electric company or dealer will be glad to show you many others. You'll find that there are beautiful, useful and *lasting* Hotpoint gifts at prices to meet every allowance on your Christmas list.

Hotpoint

EDISON ELECTRIC APPLIANCE CO., Inc.
5600 West Taylor Street   Chicago, Illinois
A GENERAL ELECTRIC   ORGANIZATION
Factories: Chicago, Illinois   and Ontario, California

Hotpoint "Ambassador" Waffle Iron

A glorious surprise awaits the one who receives this beautiful gift. In the package is a book of "52 Recipes," including cookies, shortcakes, sandwiches, corn cake and a variety of waffles. All can be made right at the table. Finished in untarnishing Hotpoint Chromeplate, with mottled green handles, $18.50. Another Chromeplate model is $12.50. Others, $9.45 and $15.00. All have the practically indestructible CALROD element.

Hotpoint 2-Slice *Automatic* Toaster with the new Toast-Over Knob

"Tell me how you like your toast and I'll make it for you *perfectly* every time—without watching, without burning." Merely put in two large slices, set the adjustable time control, and forget it. The toast will be done exactly right *automatically*. With the new Toast-Over Knob, just a twist of the wrist turns two slices at once. Hotpoint Chromeplate, $9.75. Other models, $3.95 to $9.00.

Hotpoint Super *Automatic* Iron "The Iron with a Brain"

Tell it what heat you want, by setting the throttle, and it *keeps* at that heat—low, medium, high or *any* heat between. Thus it protects your garments. It irons faster, for you never need wait for it to heat up or cool down. It also has the comfortable Thumb Rest, Hinged Plug, Heel Stand and practically indestructible CALROD element. Untarnishing Hotpoint Chromeplate, $8.80.

UNIVERSAL

SUPPER SET with Combination Sandwich Toaster and Waffle Maker

TOASTING SANDWICHES

TWO PLATE SURFACE COOKING

WAFFLE BAKING

SINGLE PLATE COOKING

Here the modern hostess is provided with an unfailing means of catering to the various tastes of her guests. It is a certain arouser of jaded appetites and drooping spirits, for foods reach their tastiest perfection when served from so smart an ensemble. Includes No. E8360 Chromium Plated, Combination Sandwich Toaster, Waffle Maker and Griddle, which has a capacity to care for the needs of almost every informal gathering; Walnut Tray, size 24½ x 15½ in., made of three-ply Walnut, will not warp, resists acid and alcohol and may be washed with soap and water; 5-Compartment Crystal Clear Glass Dish 6¼ x 14½ in.; Walnut Cutting Block, 4¾ x 14¼ in.; Cutting Knife, 7 in. Stainless Steel Blade, Ivoroy Grained Handle. 6 ft. cord.

No. E88360	Supper Set Complete	Each $24.00
No. E8360	Sandwich Toaster and Waffle Maker Only	Each $13.20

Electrovac Coffee Maker

Good Coffee Always Wanted — Here are Two Ways to Make the Best

Since most of us do depend on coffee for stimulation and relaxation, too— and since many of us drink coffee several times each day, and every day in the year, is it not important that coffee should always be served at its best, made exactly to one's taste.

New Normandie Percolator Set

Fine value at extremely low price. Exceptionally well constructed stove to give long and efficient service. Both Bowls are made of Heat-Resisting Glass. All metal parts are Chromium Plated. Black Handles and Feet. 6 foot cord.

No. E6514	Capacity 4 Cups.	Each $6.60
No. E6516	Capacity 6 Cups.	Each $6.60
No. E6518	Capacity 8 Cups.	Each $6.60

A Percolator Set of luxurious grace that adds an air of distinction to any table setting. Chromium Plated Diamond Luster Finish. New Design Dripless Spout with Black Bakelite Handle and Feet. 7 Cup Capacity. Tray 9½ x 16 inches. 6 foot cord and Safety Fuse Plug. Built with all the UNIVERSAL features that stand for perfect coffee and long life.

No. E730704	Set Complete	Each $17.30
No. E7307	Percolator only	Each $ 9.20

THESE GOODS SOLD ONLY TO MERCHANTS

For Reference Only – Original Prices Shown

UNIVERSAL
TWIN WAFFLE MAKER

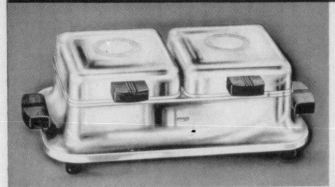

WALNUT HILL PATTERN

A New Waffle Maker in the popular Walnut Hill Pattern that bakes generous size twin waffles. Each cover has the dependable UNIVERSAL expansion hinge that permits batter to rise. Equipped with Heat Indicator and Fast 750 Watt Unit. Tray base is designed to catch any overflow of batter. Separate Aluminum Top Grids 5 x 5¾ inches. Chromium Plated. Solid Walnut Handles and Feet. 6 foot cord.

No. E8204   Each $10.30

ELECTROVAC COFFEE MAKERS

These Coffee Sets offer a simple and easy way to make Vacuum Drip Coffee — a way that leaves the coffee free from grounds or the rancid oils that are often released when boiling water comes in contact with the grounds. Heat-Resisting Glass Bowls. All metal Chromium Plated. Electric Heating Unit is a miniature reproduction of the unit made famous by the UNIVERSAL Electric Range. Creamer and Sugar Bowl, 8 oz. capacity. Tray 16 inches long has Chromium Rim and Red or Black Enamel Base to match trimming of coffee maker. Watts 550.

COMPLETE SETS

| No. E31604 | 6 Cup Capacity | Black Trimmings | Each $18.10 |
| No. E51604 | 6 Cup Capacity | Red Trimmings | Each 18.10 |

COFFEE MAKERS ONLY

Red Trim			Black Trim		
No. E514	4 Cups	Each $7.70	No. E314	4 Cups	Each $7.70
No. E516	6 Cups	Each 7.70	No. E316	6 Cups	Each 7.70
No. E518	8 Cups	Each 7.70	No. E318	8 Cups	Each 7.70

BELL-SIGNAL TOASTER

Automatically rings the bell when toast is ready and switches the current from a toasting heat to a low serving heat which keeps toast warm until toast rack is manually opened. Ideal for "Melba" toast. Adjustable for light, medium or dark toast. Chromium Finish. Bakelite Handles and Feet. Takes slice of bread 4 x 4¾ inches. For A.C. only.

No. E7122   Watts 800   Each $12.90

STREAMLINED WRINKLE-PROOF IRON

This Modern Streamline UNIVERSAL has a 20% larger ironing surface yet is no heavier than other light and standard weight irons. Round Heel, Wrinkle-Proof. Non-Skid, Knurled Heel Rest. Air Cooled, Easy Grip Bakelite Handle. Chromium Plated. Fast Heating Unit. Finger-Tip Automatic Heat Control also cuts off current — a great convenience. Six foot permanently attached cord with spring coil protection. For A.C. only.

| No. E7866 | Standard Weight | 800 Watts | Each $10.30 |
| No. E7163 | Lightweight | 1000 Watts | Each 10.30 |

9

Westinghouse Paneled Loving Cup Coffee Set

Westinghouse Marda Lamps

Westinghouse Rectigon (Battery Charger)

Westinghouse Waffle Iron

Westinghouse Table Stove

Westinghouse Curling Iron

Turnover Toaster

Westinghouse Junior Cabinet Electric Range

Merry Christmas

Let This SANTA CLAUS Present Your Gift

Let this Santa Claus, just as he smiles at you from this page, present your gift and the Christmas greeting that goes with it. He will add to the appreciation of the Grecian Urn Percolator Set, the useful Waffle Iron, or any of the other beautiful, practical Westinghouse Appliances you may select.

Worthwhile gifts every one of them—the table appliances so helpful each day at meal time, the convenient Cozy Glow, the Electric Iron, the Warming Pad for the emergency. And surely *she* understands the superiority of the Westinghouse Curling Iron!

Quality is evident throughout the Westinghouse Line, from the artistic *design* of each individual appliance to the *durability* that prepares them for hard daily usage.

It will pay you to shop early—where they sell Westinghouse Electrical Appliances.

Santa, a novel figure, just six inches tall, is specially constructed to hold in his hands your personal gift card. He is given free with each Westinghouse purchase to make the actual presentation for you on Christmas Day.

WESTINGHOUSE ELECTRIC & MANUFACTURING COMPANY
Offices in all Principal Cities · Representatives Everywhere
Tune in with KDKA—KYW—WBZ—KFKX

Westinghouse

© 1924, by the Westinghouse

Early 1918 Hotpoint Items

$50+

$50+

$50+

Chafing Dish Catalog Illustrations

ELECTRIC CHAFING SETS

Three pint chafing dish set with fine mahogany tray, spoon and fork and three bottles, castor, with silver plated tops.

Sold in 1918   **$100+ set**

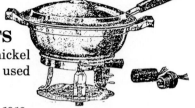

ELECTRIC CHAFING SETS

Three pints, 6 inch stove, nickel plated chafing dish. Stoves can be used with other utensils.   **$50+**

Sold in 1918

ELECTRIC CHAFING DISH

Three pints, 6 inch stove, nickel plated, 500 watts. Complete with a 6ft. cord and lamp socket connection.   **$60+**

Sold in 1918

CHAFING DISH

Nickel plated, copper body, heavily tinned and silver plated inside, ebonized wood handles and knobs, two heats, complete with 6ft. cord.   **$40+**

Sold in 1920

ELECTRIC CHAFING DISH

With a detachable stove, 9 inches diameter. Capacity is 3 pints. Diameter of stove is 6 inches. This dish has three different heat levels, nickel plated.   **$70+**

Sold in 1918

UNIVERSAL CHAFING DISH

Solid copper body, highly polished and nickel plated, inside of food pans are lined with pure tin and silver finished. Ebonized handles, feet and knobs. Heating element fitted with two heat connections, equipped with patented safety fuse plug. Complete with six foot of mercerized cord and lamp socket plug.   **$50+**

Sold in 1922

UNIVERSAL CHAFING DISH

Body is made of solid copper, nickel plated finish. Inside of food pans is lined with tin and silver finished. Ebonized handles, feet and knobs. Complete with 6ft. mercerized cord and lamp socket plug.

Sold in 1922
$50+

Sold in 1928

UNIVERSAL CHAFING DISH SET

Made of copper, with ebonized handles and knobs. The tray is 14 inches in diameter. The chafer has two heats, fast and slow. The capacity of the dish is 3 pints.   **set $75+**

CHAFING DISH / DISC STOVE

This two heat, nickel plated chafing dish is high polished with a clamping device securing water or food pan to the surface of the stove. Ebonized handles and knobs, fiber feet. Complete with 6ft. silk cord and lamp socket plug.

Sold in 1925   **$50+**

Early 1918 Hotpoint Items

$35+

Coffee Pots

$70+

Early 1918 Hotpoint Items

Coffee Pot – $20+

Tea Pot – $20+

Coffee Pot Catalog Illustrations

GOLD SEAL PERCOLATORS

Aluminum percolator having a long-life nichrome element. A keep-cool handle of neat design. Comes with a 6 ft. cord and a two-piece plug. (Shown is an 8 cup also came in a 10 cup).

$20+

Sold in 1930

COLONIAL PERCOLATOR

Eight cup, paneled design percolator, made of highly polished quality aluminum. Furnished with complete cord and plug, 110 volts.

$30+   *Sold in 1930*

GOLD SEAL URN PERCOLATOR

This percolator has a capacity of 10 cups and comes complete with cord and plug.

$35+

Sold in 1930

HOTPOINT PERCOLATOR WITH MATCHING CREAMER & SUGAR

Grecian panel design, percolator set consisting of 9 cup, 400 watt percolator wired complete, sugar, creamer and tray.

$125+   *Sold in 1930*

HOTPOINT PERCOLATOR

Copper finished in nickel, has a Calrod heating unit and fuse plug for protection of percolator.

$20+

Sold in 1930

WAAGE "REKIO" PERCOLATOR

Eight cup capacity, ebonized handle. Heating unit will last for years with ordinary care.

$30+

Sold in 1930

DOVER TABLE PERCOLATOR

The heating unit is Vea NO-BURN-OUT. Resistance coils permanently sealed against air and moisture, the only elements that can cause burn-outs.

The body is made of heavy gauge copper, polished nickel finish. All joints crimped and soldered. Comes with an unbreakable glass top, black rubberoid wood handle, and a silk cord.

Protected by fuse against discoloration or overheating. Fuse replaceable in a moment – exactly as an electric light bulb.

Sold in 1930   **$25+**

Coffee Pot Catalog Illustrations

UNIVERSAL COFFEE URN SETS

Nickel plated coffee urn, No. 440 nickel plated gold lined sugar bowl and cream pitcher and No. 440 nickel plated tray.

The urn is equipped with a safety fuse plug and a 6 ft. heater cord – (9 Cup Capacity).

Sold in 1928

$125+

URN SET FARMINGTON

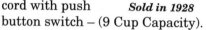

Silver overlaid and solid nickel silver butler finish. Set consists of No. 8259S urn, No. 85400 gold lined sugar bowl and cream pitcher and No. 85400 tray. Urn is equipped with a safety fuse plug and a 6ft. heater cord with push button switch – (9 Cup Capacity).

Sold in 1928　　**$140+**

ELECTRIC PERCOLATOR

Three pint capacity or eight cups, nickel plated, with stove attached.　**$20+**

Sold in 1918

ELECTRIC PERCOLATOR

Percolator with stove attached. Three pint capacity or 8 cups. Nickel plated, complete with cord and lamp socket connection.

Sold in 1918

$70+

ELECTRIC PERCOLATOR

Percolator with a capacity of three pints or 8 cups. Equipped with patent fusible nut, which disconnects the current in case it is allowed to boil dry. Complete with cord and lamp socket.

Sold in 1918　**$20+**

ELECTRIC PERCOLATOR

A capacity of three pints or eight cups, nickel plated, with 6 ft. of cord and lamp socket connection.

Sold in 1918

$35+

Coffee Pot Catalog Illustrations

PERCOLATOR

Nickel plated, copper body, tinned and silver-plated inside. With ebonized handles, and a 6ft. cord.

$20+ *Sold in 1920*

COFFEE URN

Tudor pattern urn, 14½ inches, 6 cups, nickel plated. Has ebonized handles, complete with 6ft. of mercerized cord.

$55+

Sold in 1920

PERCOLATOR

Six cup pot, 9½ inches, nickel plated, ebonized handle and feet, colonial pattern, complete with 6ft. of mercerized cord.

$20+

Sold in 1920

COFFEE URN

Colonial style, 13½ inches high, 6 cups capacity, nickel plated, ebonized handles, complete with 6ft. of mercerized cord, 110 volts.

$55+

Sold in 1920

COFFEE URN

Loving cup pattern, 15½ inches high, 6 cup capacity. Nickel plated, ebonized handles, complete with 6ft. of ebonized cord.

$70+

Sold in 1920

PERCOLATOR

Eight cup aluminum percolator with ebonized handle, complete with a 6ft. cord, 11½ inches high.

Sold in 1920   **$20+**

PERCOLATOR

Seven cups, nickel plated, ebonized handle. Complete with a 6ft. cord.

$20+

Sold in 1920

PERCOLATOR

Seven cup, 11 inch percolator. Nickel plated, ebonized handles, complete with 6ft. of cord.

$35+

Sold in 1920

Coffee Pot Catalog Illustrations

PERCOLATOR

Colonial pattern, nickel plated, 10¼ inches high, 8 cup, ebonized handles, complete with 6ft of cord.

$20+

Sold in 1920

PERCOLATOR

Ten cup percolator, 11¼ inches high, nickel plated, ebonized handles. Complete with 6ft of cord.

$20+

Sold in 1920

PERCOLATOR

Urn type, 16 inches, 8 cups, nickel plated, mahoganite handles, complete with 6ft. cord.

$70+

Sold in 1920

PERCOLATOR

Urn type, 11½ inches, 7 cup, nickel plated percolator with ebonized handles. Complete with 6ft. cord.

$35+

Sold in 1920

PERCOLATOR

Seven cup, 11½ inch high, nickel plated percolator with mahoganite handles. Complete with 6ft. of cord.

Sold in 1920

$35+

PERCOLATOR

Ten cup percolator, 11¼ inches high, nickel plated, ebonized handles. Complete with 6ft of cord.

$35+

Sold in 1920

PERCOLATOR

Ten cup, 11¾ inches high, copper percolator with mahoganite handles. Complete with a 6ft. cord.

$35+

Sold in 1920

PERCOLATOR SET

A four piece nickel plated percolator set. Ten cup, 11¾ inches high, 16 inches oblong waiter, gold lines cream and sugar, mahoganite handles. Complete with a 6ft cord.

Sold in 1920   **$125+**

Coffee Pot Catalog Illustrations

UNIVERSAL

Six cup, 9¹ᐟ² inch, nickel plated, ebonized handle, colonial pattern. Complete with 6ft. mercerized cord.

$20+ *Sold in 1920*

UNIVERSAL SAMOVAR

Six cup, 11³ᐟ⁴ inches, nickel plated, ebonized handles and knobs, complete with 6ft. mercerized cord.

$35+

Sold in 1920

PERCOLATOR MANNING-BOWMAN

Seven cup, nickel plated, copper body, with ebonized handles. Complete with 6ft. cord.

Sold in 1920   **$20+**

UNIVERSAL MILK WARMER

Nickel plated, 110 volts, ebonized handles and feet. For warming liquids at an even temperature it cannot be excelled.

Sold in 1920   **$15+**

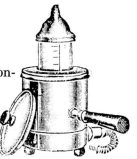

MAJESTIC PERCOLATOR

Made of rolled copper, heavily nickel plated. 9¹ᐟ² inches high, 2¹ᐟ² pints capacity. Cool ebony finish wood handle. Furnished with a 6ft. cord and plug.

Sold in 1921   **$20+**

DE LUXE COFFEE URN

Body is made of rolled copper, nickel plated. Stands 15 inches tall and measures 10¹ᐟ⁴ inches between handles. Holds 2¹ᐟ² pints or about six cups. Furnished with a 6ft. cord and plug.   **$65+**

Sold in 1921

ELECTRIC PERCOLATOR

This percolator is highly polished with ebonized wood handle, and a 6ft. cord with attaching plug. Holds 9 cups, uses 450 watts, for use on 108 to 120 current.

Sold in 1922   **$25+**

UNIVERSAL GRECIAN PATTERN

Heavy gauge nickel plated copper body, ivoroy faucet handle and feet, heat proof cut glass top. Inside is coated with pure tin, silver finish, aluminum interior fittings, complete with a 6ft. mercerized silk cord and lamp socket plug.

$60+

Sold in 1922

Coffee Pot Catalog Illustrations

URN COFFEE POT

Seven cup urn, nickel plated, with metal handles.

$35+

Sold in 1925

HOTPOINT PERCOLATOR

This paneled design pot is copper, nickel plated with ebonized handles, fibre feet, hinged cover. Inside is silver finished. Fitted with standard valveless percolating apparatus and safety switch, which breaks current on the change of voltage, or if pot goes dry to prevent burnouts. Complete with cord (16CD6) attachment plug and interchangeable connecting plug.

Sold in 1926

$25+

HOTPOINT PERCOLATOR

This colonial designed percolator is copper, nickel plated with ebonized handles, fibre feet, hinged colating apparatus and safety switch, which breaks current on change of voltage, or if pot goes dry it prevents burnouts. Cord attachment plug and interchangeable connecting plug, (cord 16CD6).

Sold in 1926

$20+

HOTPOINT PERCOLATOR

This Grecian designed percolator is copper, nickel plated, ebonized handles, fibre feet, hinged cover with a silver finish inside. Fitted with standard valveless percolating apparatus and safety switch, cord attachment plug and interchangeable connecting plug, (cord 16CD6).

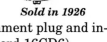

Sold in 1926

$20+

HOTPOINT PERCOLATOR

Pure seamless aluminum with an ebonized wood handle. Flanged rim cover locked by slight turn. Outside finish is highly polished, inside is satin. Has a standard valveless percolating apparatus and safety switch, cord attachment plug and interchangeable connecting plug, (cord 16CD6).

Sold in 1926

$20+

THERMAX PERCOLATOR

The body of this percolator is spun from pure aluminum, nichrome wire heating element, ebonized handle. Complete with a 6ft. of silk connecting cord and separable attachment plug, and a safety fuse plug to prevent overheating of element.

Sold in 1926

$20+

Coffee Pot Catalog Illustrations

EDISON PERCOLATOR
Buffed aluminum, glass top, welded spout, and ebonized handle with cord and plug.

$20+

Sold in 1926

BLUE LINE COFFEE POT
A paneled body percolator, 8 cup capacity. Made of heavy gauge aluminum rubbed to a mirror-like finish, ebonized handle and fiber tipped feet. Complete with 6ft of cord and plug.

Sold in 1927

$20+

BERSTED ELECTRIC PERCOLATOR
This nine cup percolator is 110 volts. Made of heavy gauge aluminum, highly polished, nichrome heating element with heat resisting glass top and ebonized handles. Complete with 6ft of cord with separable attachment plug and detachable contact plug.

Sold in 1927

$20+

Sold in 1927

UNIVERSAL ELECTRIC MONTICELLO PATTERN FOUR PIECE PERCOLATING SET
Nickel plated on copper, metal handles, fibre ball feet, ebony faucet handle. 12 x 18 inch octagon tray with metal handles. Capacity of Urn is 4 pints or 9 cups.

$150+

Sold in 1927

$150+

UNIVERSAL ELECTRIC OLD ENGLISH PATTERN DE LUXE PERCOLATOR SET
Nickel plated on copper, cut glass top, ivoroy feet-handle-and knobs. Capacity of Urn is 4 pints or 9 cups.

UNIVERSAL ELECTRIC LEXINGTON PATTERN FOUR-PIECE PERCOLATING SET
Nickel plated on copper, ebonized handle and feet, 14 inch round tray. Capacity of Percolator is 3 pints or 6 cups.

$65+

Sold in 1927

Coffee Pot Catalog Illustrations

UNIVERSAL ELECTRIC MARIE ANTOINETTE PATTERN FOUR PIECE PERCOLATING URN SET

Nickel plated on copper with metal handles, fibre ball feet, ebony faucet handles. Oval tray is 13 x 20 inches, capacity of urn is 4 pints or 9 cups.

$100+

Sold in 1927

ELECTRIC ALUMINUM COFFEE PERCOLATOR

Made of heavy aluminum, finely polished with ebonized handles, one-piece spout brazed to the body. Capacity is 6 cups or 3 pints. Also available in 9 cups or 4 pints .

Sold in 1927

$15+

COLONIAL PATTERN PERCOLATOR

This percolator is silver overlaid with a satin finish. Capacity is 3 pints or 6 cups.

$35+

Sold in 1927

CAVALIER PATTERN COFFEE PERCOLATING URN SET

Silver overlaid on solid nickel silver, with a satin finish. Metal handles, ebonized feet and faucet handles. The capacity of the urn is 4 pints or 9 cups.

Sold in 1927

$150+

Sold in 1927

$130+

MANNING BOWMAN PERCOLATOR SET

Butler finished, nickel silver, silver plated percolator set with repousse chased design on all pieces. Capacity of percolator is 9 cups.

Coffee Pot Catalog Illustrations

**ATHENIAN PATTERN
PERCOLATING URN SET**

Hammered design silver overlaid on solid nickel silver, with metal handles, ivoroy feet and faucet handle. Capacity of urn is 4 pints or 9 cups.

$70+

Sold in 1927

**ATHENIAN PATTERN
PERCOLATING URN SET**

Silver overlaid on solid nickel silver, metal handles, ivoroy feet and faucet handles. 13 x 20 inch oval tray. The urn has a capacity of 4 pints or 9 cups.

Sold in 1927   **$70+**

Sold in 1927

**UNIVERSAL GRECIAN PATTERN
URN SET**

Silver plated, butler finish, Decorative chased bands, ivoroy faucet, handles and feet, and a cut glass top. The tray is 13 x 18 inches.

$125+

Sold in 1927

**UNIVERSAL WESTMINSTER
PATTERN URN SET**

Silver overlaid on nickel silver with a butler french grey finish. A cut glass top and ivory feet, knob and handles. The capacity is 9 cups, the tray size is 12 x 18 inches.

$150+

Coffee Pot Catalog Illustrations

MANNING BOWMAN URN SET

Colonial design, butler silver plated. The urn has a capacity of 9 cups, with an 18 inch oval tray with handles.

Sold in 1927

$125+

HOTPOINT "PLYMOUTH" ELECTRIC PERCOLATOR

Puritan design, 6 cups, drawn copper body, full nickel plated, beaded spout, fuse type "Calrod" heating element, with cord and plug.

Sold in 1928

$20+

ROME ELECTRIC PERCOLATOR

Nickel plated solid copper, 8 cup percolator. Eleven inches high, seamed spout, hot water type, black enameled dull finish handle with cord and

Sold in 1928

plugs. Complete with a sugar and creamer and a 12 inch tray to match. **$50+**

ROME ELECTRIC PERCOLATOR

Nickel plated solid copper, 8 cup percolator, 11 inches high, 1-pc. spout, cold water type, black enameled dull finish handle. "Smith" switch plug at base with cord and plugs. Complete with a sugar and creamer and a 12 inch tray to match.

Sold in 1928

$50+

HOTPOINT ELECTRIC PERCOLATOR

Nickel plated solid copper, 6 cup percolator, sheath wire heating unit, fuse plug with cord. Complete with a sugar and creamer and a 14 inch tray to match.

Sold in 1928

$50+

SWANSTON PATTERN PERCOLATOR

Heavily nickel plated percolator, ebonized wood handle, fiber feet, equipped with gravity reset safety switch, 350 watts, 7 ft. flexible cord and plug. No. H22124 has a capacity of 3 cups, No. H22125's capacity is 5 cups.

Sold in 1928

$20+

Coffee Pot Catalog Illustrations

MARIE ANTOINETTE PERCOLATOR SET

The urn is 13$^{1/2}$ inches high, with a white faucet and feet, 9 cup capacity, is equipped with the gravity reset, safety switch, 7ft of flexible cord and plug, 350 watts. Complete with Creamer and Sugar and an 18 inch oval tray.

$200+

Sold in 1928

LOUIS XIV PATTERN PERCOLATOR SET

The urn is 14 inches high, with white handles and feet, 9 cup capacity, equipped with gravity reset safety switch, 7ft. cord and plug, 350 watts.

Sold in 1928   **$175+**

LOUIS XIV PERCOLATOR

Nickel plated electric percolator, 13 inches high, equipped with a gravity reset safety switch, 359 watt. Complete with a 7ft. flexible cord and plug, 7 cup capacity.   **$40+**

Sold in 1928

Sold in 1928

EARLY AMERICAN PERCOLATOR SET

The urn is 13$^{1/4}$ inches high, equipped with gravity reset safety switch, 350 watts, 7 ft. flexible cord and plug. 7 cup capacity. Complete with a sugar, creamer and a 14 inch tray.   **$125+**

EARLY AMERICAN PERCOLATOR

Nickel plated, 111/2 inches high, ebonized wood handle, fiber feet, 7 cup capacity. Equipped with the gravity reset safety switch, 350 watts, 7ft. flexible cord and plug.   **$20+**

Sold in 1928

Coffee Pot Catalog Illustrations

EARLY AMERICAN PERCOLATOR

Nickel plated, 11½ inches high, ebonized wood handle, fiber feet, 7 cup capacity. Equipped with the gravity reset safety switch, 350 watts, 7ft. flexible cord and plug.

$65+

Sold in 1928

HOMELECTRIC PERCOLATOR

This 7 cup capacity percolator, highly nickel plated on copper, has a non-heating ebonized wood handle. A fuse link protector which prevents damage to percolator if the current is turned on when pot is empty. **$20+**

Sold in 1928

OLD ENGLISH PATTERN PERCOLATOR

Chromium plate, blue diamond finish, ivoroy antique feet and ivory antique casein insulator handle. Capacity is 6 cups. **$35+**

Sold in 1929

OLD ENGLISH PATTERN COFFEE PERCOLATOR SET

Chromium plate blue diamond finish, ivoroy antique handles, faucet, and feet. Push button switch attachment plug. The urn has the capacity of 9 cups. The tray size is 12 x 18 inches.

$150+

Sold in 1929

Coffee Pot Catalog Illustrations

LAFAYETTE PATTERN ELECTRIC COFFEE PERCOLATOR SET

Chromium plate, blue diamond finish with ivoroy pennant handles and faucet handle, fibre feet. The capacity of the urn is 9 cups, the tray is 12 x 18 inches, equipped with push button switch attachment plug.

$175+

Sold in 1929

PERCOLATOR

This fluted aluminum buffed, 4 cup capacity percolator is highly polished with fiber tipped feet, black curved handle.

Sold in 1931

$20+

ROYAL ROCHESTER ELECTRIC PERCOLATOR SET

The "Golden Pheasant" design, is made of heat proof china. Metal mountings. The tray is made of heavy lustrous royal nickel plate. Handles of tray are trimmed with white erinoid. Capacity of percolator is 7 cups.

Sold in 1929   **$175+**

EXTRACTOLATOR COFFEE MAKER

Finished in sparkling chromium plate, trimmed in jet black, coffee maker never boils the coffee so there is no bitter flavors. It throws the correct volume of water over the coffee at the correct temperature to extract all the rich flavor. Complete with the easy-pouring handle, non-drip spout, fuse-protected heating element, with cord and full direction.

$45+

Sold in 1934

Sold in 1934

UNIVERSAL COFFEE MAKER ELECTROVAC

Chromium plated copper body, tinned inside, extra heavy polished heat-proof glass bowl protected by heavy rubber gasket. Equipped with ivoroy handles, knobs and feet, and a faucet for convenient serving, nichrome heating unit. Complete with six feet of art silk cord and plugs.

$60+

Coffee Pot Catalog Illustrations

G.E. HOTPOINT "MOHAWK" COFFEE MAKER

Makes clear, sparkling, rich flavored coffee. The pyrex bowls are guaranteed against breakage from heat. The metal parts are finished in gleaming chrome plate with black textolite handles and has a glow coil element, complete with cord.

$60+

Sold in 1935

VACUUM DRIP COFFEE MAKER

This coffee maker does not release tannin or oils in the coffee, with a patented glass filter, no metal touches the coffee. Bowls are made of a heat resisting "glassbake". Finely ground coffee is used. Complete with electric stove.

Sold in 1937 **$45+**

Sold in 1938

MODERN COFFEE SERVICE

$250+

This 12 cup urn does double duty, after lifting out the percolating parts, it becomes a 16 cup coffee server. Protected against overheating by a thermostatic control, it is chromium finished, with black trimmings.

WHITE CROSS COFFEE-VAC TRAY SET

Has triple speed sanitary filter, installed and removed in a flash. The glass will withstand great heat and other important features make White Cross outstanding. Complete with platinum banded glass units with decanter cover, all equipped with bakelite handles.

$90+

Sold in 1938

Sold in 1939

COFFEE PERCOLATORS, DEVONSHIRE PATTERN

Chromium plated copper body, with a silver finish inside. The aluminum interior fittings, heat-proof glass top, pump and spreader plate percolating system, nichrome heating element protected by a safety fuse plug, mahogany composition handle and feet, with an art silk cord and plug.

$25+

Sold in 1939

PERCOLATOR COFFEE SERVICE

The spherical shape of the percolator with its perky spout is very distinctive. Finished in gleaming chromium plate with a white handle. Matching sugar and creamer. **$175+**

Coffee Pot Catalog Illustrations

VISULATOR COFFEE-MAKER

Designed in heat-resisting insured glass by Corning Glass Works, hand decorated with platinum stripes. Coffee can be brewed to any strength desired. Chromium plated with ebony finished handles.

$125+

Sold in 1939

URN AUTOMATIC

A electric marvel coffee drip urn. Current automatically shuts off when coffee is properly brewed. Low heat unit keeps it hot until ready to serve. A chromium plated finish with black handles and a heat resisting glass bowl.

$60+

Sold in 1939

FARBERWARE COFFEE ROBOT AUTOMATIC COFFEE-MAKER

This Coffee Robot stirs automatically while brewing, and makes the coffee exactly right then shuts off, but keeps it hot and fresh until served. Complete with sugar, creamer and tray to match.

$110+

Sold in 1941

Coffee Pots

CORY COFFEE MAKER

Model DEO, chrome with black bakelite handles, 660 watts, 115 volts AC/DC. By Cory Glass Coffee Brewer Co., Chicago, IL.

$45+

1942 G.E. AUTOMATIC COFFEE MAKER

Chrome, bakelite and glass, with red and black bakelite handles, 750 watts, 115 volts. By General Electric Co., Bridgeport, CT. (This appliance has never been used and still has the sales tag on it. Possibly patented in 1942 but wasn't sold until the end of WWII, 1946). **$125+**

1938 HOTPOINT "DORCHESTER" COFFEE MAKER

Chrome and glass with black bakelite handles, 550 watts, 115 volts. By General Electric Co.

$65+

1940 G.E. AUTOMATIC COFFEE MAKER

Chrome, bakelite and glass, with black bakelite handles, 115 volts. By General Electric, Bridgeport, CT. (The upper handle locks onto the upper bowl and can be inverted to serve as stand while the lower pot is serving coffee).

$125+

Coffee Pots

CORY COFFEE MAKER

Model D.E.O., glass with plastic handle and chrome heater and porcelain insert, 13" tall, 660-80 w/115 volts. By Glass Coffee Brewer Corp., Chicago, IL.

$35+

MID 1930'S FARBERWARE COFFEE MAKER

Model #10, chrome and glass with painted wood handles, 425 watts, and 115 volts. By S.W. Farber Inc., Brooklyn, NY.

$75+

1935 SILEX COFFEE MAKER

Model #LE-82, chrome, glass and black bakelite handles, 525 watts. By The Silex Co., Hartford, CT.

$55+

1934 ELECTRO-BREW

Model #70, glass (made by Pyrex) and bakelite with stainless steel lid, 115 volts, 300 watt. By Coleman Lamp & Stove Co., Wichita, KS.

$60+

Coffee Pots

1950's SUNBEAM COFFEE MAKER
Model #C50, chrome and bakelite with black bakelite handles, 1140 watts, 120 volts. By Sunbeam Corp., Chicago, IL. The standing is for holding the top while serving the coffee.
$30+

1951 KNAPP-MONARCH COFFEE MAKER
The body is made of chrome with brown bakelite handles, 800 watts. By Knapp-Monarch, St. Louis, MO.
$30+

1944 SUNBEAM COFFEE MASTER
Model C30, Deco design chrome with bakelite handles and base, 1000 watts, 120 volts, 12½" tall. By Sunbeam Corporation, Chicago.
$40+

1925 MANNING-BOWMAN COFFEE MAKER
Model 39717, chrome body with a wood handle, 350 watts, 110-120 volts, 11" tall. By Manning-Bowman & Co., Meridan, CT., U.S.A.
$30+

Coffee Pots

1925 MERIDEN HOMELECTRICS COFFEE BREWER

Pewter body with a wood handle, 11" tall, 115 volts, 400 watts. By Manning-Bowman & Co., Meriden, Ct, U.S.A.

$30+

HOTPOINT CALROD COFFEE MAKER

Chrome body with black bakelite handle, 115 volts, 400 watts. By General Electric.

$20+

CORY COFFEE POT

Model ACB, chrome body with black bakelite handle, 800 watts. By Cory Corp., Chicago, IL.

$25+

1937 CORY COFFEE POT

Model DEA, chrome body with bakelite handle, 800 watts. By Cory Corp., Chicago, IL.

$25+

Coffee Pots

1955 G.E. AUTOMATIC PERCOLATOR

Chrome body with brown bakelite handle, 800 watts. By General Electric Co.

$15+

1955 SUNBEAM COFFEEMASTER AUTOMATIC PERCOLATOR

Model AP10A, chrome body and black bakelite handle, 600 watts. By Sunbeam Corp., Chicago, IL.

$20+

1942 COFFEE "FORMAN" MAID BREWER

Chromium on solid brass, plastic handle and feet, 110-115 volts, 550 watts, 10¾" tall. By Forman Family. The glass insert is by Pyrex.

$55+

COLOR GLO FLAVO-MATIC AUTOMATIC ELECTRIC PERCOLATOR

Blue coffee pot with white plastic handle, 8 cup capacity, 110-120 volts, 400 watts, 9 1/2" tall x 6" dia. Complete with original box. By West Bend Aluminum Co.

$35+

Coffee Pots

FARBERWARE AUTOMATIC COFFEE MAKER

Model 500, chrome with wood handles and feet, 120 volts, 550 watts, 14¼" tall. Patented 1937, by S.W. Farber Inc., Brooklyn, NY.

$45+

MANNING BOWMAN AUTOMATIC COFFEE MAKER

Chrome body with black bakelite feet, 115 volts, 365-450 watts. By Manning-Bowman & Co., Meriden, CT.

$100+

ROYAL ROCHESTER COFFEE MAKER

Chrome body, 410 watts, fabulous high art deco design. By Robeson Rochester Corp., Rochester, NY. A brewing selector had been built into the base for selecting the number of cups percolated.   **$100+**

ART DECO COFFEE MAKER

This round coffee maker is chrome with yellow bakelite accents, patented 1925, 110-120 volts, 380 watts, 14¾" tall. By Manning-Bowman & Co., Meriden, CT.

$125+

Coffee Pots

FARBERWARE COFFEE BREWER
Chrome with painted wood handles and feet, patented 1932, 13¾" tall. By S.W. Farber, Inc., Brooklyn, NY.

$25+

CONTINENTAL COFFEE BREWER
The body is made of chrome with bakelite handles and wooden feet, 115 volts, 400 watts, 14" tall. By Continental Silver Co., Inc.

$25+

1924 UNIVERSAL COFFEE PERCULATOR
Chrome with ivory handle and green depression glass lid, 108-116 volts, 420 watts, 10½" tall x 7" dia. By Landers Frary & Clark, New Britain, CT.

$85+

1925 MERIDEN HOMELECTRICS COFFEE PERCULATOR
Chrome with wood handles, 110 volts, 400 watts, 13¼" tall. By Manning-Bowman, Meriden CT.

$45+

Coffee Pots

MODEL E9169 UNIVERSAL COFFEE MAKER

Copper and brass body with wood handles and a glass insert in top, patented 1914, 115-120 volts, 3.4 amps, 16¼" tall. By Landers, Frary & Clark, New Britain, CT.

$70+

1914 UNIVERSAL COFFEE POT

Model E9189, sterling silver, brass with ivoroy handles, bottom and feet, 115-120 volts, 14" tall. By Landers, Frary & Clark, New Britain, CT.

$60+

ART DECO COFFEE MAKER

Chrome, with wood handles, with glass insert in lid.

$65+

UNIVERSAL COFFEE SET

Chrome, with black bakelite handles and feet, the brew control handle is brown bakelite, no. E4408, 110 volts, 400 watts. By Landers, Frary & Clark, New Britain. CT.

$60+

Coffee Pots

ANCHORWARE COFFEE SET
Porcelain coffee maker with creamer and sugar with painted wood feet, chrome top with glass insert, with a Champion heater.
$100+

UNITED COFFEE MAKER SET
Coffee maker, sugar and creamer made of chrome with translucent red handles, 115 volts, 550 watts. By United Metal Goods, Brooklyn, NY.
$75+

SUNBEAM COFFEE SET
Coffee maker, sugar and creamer, hot plate and tray, set #4, 110-120 volts, 50-450 watts. By Chicago Flexible Shaft Co., Chicago, IL, U.S.A.
$50+

FORMAN COFFEE SET
Coffee maker, tray, sugar, creamer, and two containers. Chrome with bakelite handles and pyrex glass insert in top, 115 volts, 450 watts. By Forman Bros. Inc., Brooklyn, NY.
$100+

Coffee Pots

1937 KITCHEN AID COFFEE MILL

Model A-9, the base is pot metal, 115 volts, 1.25 amps. By The Hobart Manufacturing Co., Troy, OH.

$70+

COFFEE SET

Coffee Urn with creamer and sugar, aluminum with lucite handles on the coffee brewer, 115 volts, 400 watts. By Continental Silver Co., Inc.

$35+

1954 SUNBEAN COFFEE SET

Model C30C, chrome body, with bakelite handle, 120 volts, 1000 watts. By Sunbeam Corporation, Chicago, IL.

$65+

Early 1918 Hotpoint Items

Table Grill
$20+

Grill Catalog Illustrations

PEERLESS GRILL

High quality construction, wired completely, element is easily replaced, 110 volts. Nickel plated.

Sold in 1930

$15+

MAJESTIC COMBINATION GRILL

Combination griddle, frying pan and broiler all made of pressed steel, nickel plated. Depth of frying pan is $1^{1/8}$ inches, broiler is 2 inches, griddle is $3/16$ of an inch. Heating surface is 7 x $3^{3/4}$ x 10 inches. Operates on any electric light circuit with the usual city current of 105 to 115 volts. *Sold in 1918*

$75+

FOUR HEAT GRILL

Full nickel plated, 3 steel cooking pans, $7^{1/2}$ inches, $1/4$, $1^{1/4}$ and 2 inches depth, ebonized wood handles with 6ft. cord.

Sold in 1920

$65+

GRILL

Nickel plated, three heat grill. Makes toast or pancakes two at a time. May also be used as a separate stove. Complete with 6ft. cord.

Sold in 1920

$65+

ELECTRIC GRILL

Heavy gauge sheet steel base and frame, nickel plated, highly polished, sheet steel pans and griddles, ebonized wood handles, heating element wound to obtain concentrated heat, complete with one frying pan, one boiling pan and one griddle and six feet of mercerized silk finish flexible cord and triple contact terminal plug.

Sold in 1922

$70+

UNIVERSAL ELECTRIC GRILLS

Nickel plated sheet steel pans with ebonized handles, fibre feet, patent element wound in three concentric circles, removable rack with four separate pans for poaching eggs. Complete with three heat snap switch, 6ft. heater cord and lamp socket plug.

Sold in 1922

$90+

HOTPOINT RADIANT GRILL

This three heat grill will broil, toast, or fry. Made of pressed steel nickel plated. Deep under-dish with grid. Shallow dish cover fits either, also serves as a reflector or cake griddle. Ordinary enameled ware utensils can also be used. Complete with cord 16CD6. Deep pan $7^{7/8}$ x $1^{7/8}$ inches, medium pan is $7^{7/8}$ x $1^{1/2}$ inches, and shallow pan is $7^{7/8}$ x $1^{1/4}$ inches. *Sold in 1926*

$65+

UNIVERSAL PANCAKE GRIDDLES

This griddle has a nickel plated base which can serve as a tray. The grid is made of pure aluminum with ebonized handles and feet. Good for making griddle cakes and also to fry bacon, eggs, etc. Complete with a 6ft. silk heated cord, push button switch and separable attachment plug.

Sold in 1928

$25+

Grill Catalog Illustrations

HOTPOINT RADIANT GRILL

This grill broils, fries and toasts, two different op- *Sold in 1926* erations at one time. Made of pressed steel, oblong shaped, nickel plated, with reflector type grid. Medium pan is $5/8$ inch, shallow pan is $1/4$ inch and used for cover for other two pans. All pans are $8\ 1/2$ x $4\ 1/4$ inch, tray is $10^{3/4}$ x $7^{1/4}$ inch.

$75+

BERSTED ELECTRIC GRIDDLE

Nickel plated, $8^{1/4}$ inch cast aluminum top, nichrome heat- *Sold in 1927* ing element with black ebony handles and fiber feet. Complete with 6ft. of super-heater cord equipped with separable attachment plug and detachable contact plug.

$20+

LITTLE WONDER ELECTRIC GRILL

Single burner, 110 volt, nickel plated, $6^{3/4}$ inches *Sold in 1928* high, 6ft of durable cord with detachable plug that will fit any lamp socket.

$15+

THOMAS A. EDISON EDICRAFT SANDWICH GRILL

Made with durable chromium, they will never tarnish

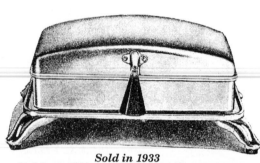

Sold in 1933

and require no polishing. This sandwich grill toasts or broils. Comes complete with a deep plate attachment which is easily fixed in place and has a drain to catch grease. Grill has bakelite handles and feet, steel construction with die cast aluminum grids and plate.

$25+

Sold in 1933

EVERHOT ELECTRIC KITCHENETTE GRILLE

For broiling, frying or boiling. Toasts eight pieces of bread at one time. Percolates coffee. Intensely hot, free of soot and odor, cooks quickly and perfectly. Aluminum pan and wire rack for broiling or toasting. Aluminum griddle for frying or making pancakes or broiling and or toasting. Three heats, controlled by two switches.

$150+

SUNBEAM GRILL AND TOASTER

This grill can be used right at the table for breakfast, luncheons, afternoon tea, for dinner

Sold in 1934

and for a light refreshment any time. It broils, bakes, frys, stews etc.

$50+

Grills

GENERAL ELECTRIC SANDWICH
Chrome with bakelite handles, patented 1935, 115 volts, 600 watts, 14½" x 9" x 4¼". By General Electric Co., Bridgeport, CT - Ontario, CA.
$25+

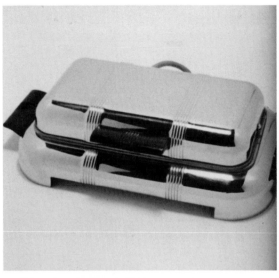

WHITE CROSS ELECTRIC GRILL
Model 228, chrome with black bakelite handles, 575 watts. By National Stamping and Electric Works, Chicago, IL.
$25+

1938 PATRICIAN ELECTRIC GRILL
Model 326, chrome and black painted metal, with black bakelite handles, 500 watts. By Bersted Manufacturing Co., Fostoria, OH.
$50+

1931 DOMINION "MODERN-MODE SANDWICH QUEEN" WAFFLE IRON
Model 510, chrome with bakelite handles, 110-120 volts, 660 watts, 15" x 4¾" x 8½". By Dominion Electrical Mfg. Co., Minneapolis, MN.
$25+

Early 1918 Hotpoint Items

$25+

Hot Plate

Hot Plate Catalog Illustrations

No. 1H4214 – HOT PLATE

Nickel plated, three heat control switch, 110 volts, with a cooking surface of 11 x 11, and $5\frac{1}{2}$ inches high. Furnished with a 6ft cord and attachment plug.

Sold in 1920

$25+

No. 1H3224 – ARMSTRONG HOT PLATE

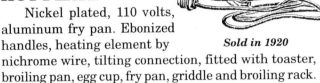

Nickel plated, 110 volts, aluminum fry pan. Ebonized handles, heating element by *Sold in 1920* nichrome wire, tilting connection, fitted with toaster, broiling pan, egg cup, fry pan, griddle and broiling rack.

$70+

No. 6F8027¹ᐟ⁴ – HOT PLATE

Used for general cooking, heating surface, $5\frac{1}{2}$ inches in diameter. This is 660-watt size and **$25+** is equipped with a three heat switch, giving full medium and low heat. *Sold in 1921* Nickel plated and polished, equipped with 6ft of hose and separable plug.

No. 631856 – SINGLE BURNER ELECTRIC HOT PLATE

Cooks or stews anything which may be cooked on any regular *Sold in 1922* stove. Maybe attached to any lamp socket. Fitted with a 6ft. cord and attaching plug. For use on 108 to 120 volts current, uses 660 watts.

$20+

No. G7162X – LIBERTY HOT PLATE

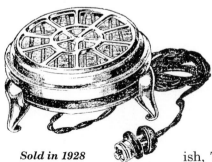

This hot plate toasts, boils, fries. Nickel finish, $7\frac{1}{2}$ inches wide, 4 *Sold in 1928* inches high, 110 volts. Coiled heating element, 38 inches, complete with cord and plug.

$20+

No. 986 – UNIVERSAL HOT PLATE

This hot plate boils, fries and stews. Nickel plated, nickeled reflector plate, and an ebonized handle. **$20+** Equipped with a 6ft. heater cord, an open coil heating unit. Diameter of the cooking top is 6 inches, 550 watts.

Sold in 1928

Hot Plate Catalog Illustrations

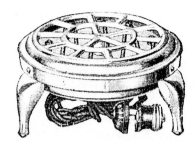

No. 701 – LIBERTY HOT PLATE

Made of 20 gauge steel frame, nickel plated. Nichrome wire heating element, easily replaced when burnt out. Equipped with a 6ft. heater cord. Diameter 7 inches, height 4 inches, 500 watts.

$20+

No. 3H – LIBERTY HOT PLATE

Frame and legs made from cast aluminum-copper alloy, highly polished, and black enamel handles. The 6 inch nichrome wire heating elements , four station switch affords full heat on either element at one time or medium heat on both elements at once. Equipped with a 6ft. heater cord. Operates from any electrical outlet. Height is 5 inches, width is 11 inches, length is 21 inches, 600 watts.

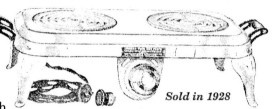

Sold in 1928

$35+

Sold in 1930

No. 701 – LIBERTY HOT PLATE

Highly nickel plated, 7 inches diameter, 4 inches high, 400 watts. Guaranteed 1 year. Wired completely, 110 volts.

$20+

No. 5H – SUPER HOT PLATE

Highly nickel plated, 7 inches diameter, 4 inches high, 400 watts. Guaranteed 1 year. Wired completely, 110 volts.

Sold in 1930

$35+

No. 601 – LIBERTY HOT SPOT

High grade construction, genuine nichrome heating element, wired complete, 110 volts.

Sold in 1930

$20+

No. CS1 – GOLD SEAL HOT PLATE

A quality plate made by one of the large manufacturers of heating devices. Nickel plated, with a nichrome heating element.

Sold in 1930

$35+

HOT PLATES

DECO HOT PLATE
Model 232A, chrome and black body, 110-120 volts, 660 watts, 9" x 9" x 4". By Electrahot Mfg. Co., Mansfield, OH.
$15+

BERSTED HOT PLATE
Model 15, chrome and metal, 115 volts, 660 watts, 8" x 4" x 8". By Bersted Mfg. Co., Fostoria, OH.
$15+

WESTINGHOUSE DOUBLE HOT PLATE
Porcelain coated, patented 1915, 110 volts, 1100 watts, 18" L x 10½" W x 5" T. By Westinghouse Electric & Manufacturing Co., Mansfield Works, Mansfield, OH.
$50+

ELECTRIC HOT PLATE TRIVET
Model TRV-1, cast iron trivet with hot plate, 120 volts, 50 watts, 43/4" x 73/4". By Paragon Electric Co., Two Rivers, WI.
$15+

WESTINGHOUSE HOT PLATE
Porcelain enameled top, 71/2" x 41/8" tall, 110 volts, 550 watts. By Westinghouse Elect. & Mfg. Co., Mansfield Works, Mansfield, OH.
$25+

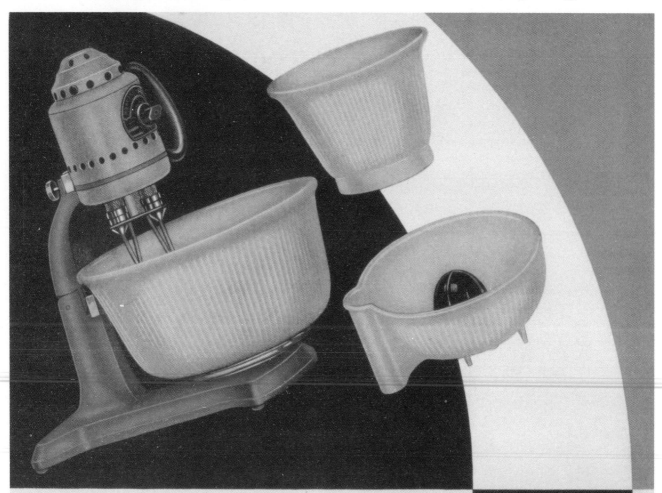

THE KITCHEN MIXER

The Kitchen Mixer is one of the greatest labor saving devices of the day. Because it is designed to do any kind of a mixing job it saves much wearying work and does it better. It actually improves your favorite recipes because it beats thoroughly. You can use it on the stand with the revolving mixing bowls or use it as a portable mixer for beating or mixing on the stove or any other place in the kitchen. It mixes all kinds of batter, mashes potatoes, whips cream, beats frostings and candies, extracts fruit juices.

One of the special features of the Manning-Bowman Kitchen Mixer is its separable paddles. This is highly important because most paddles take so long to clean. They pull apart instantly so that you can clean them quickly and thoroughly. Still another feature is its very powerful motor. It will not stall on the heaviest kitchen mixing job.

Manning-Bowman appliances are outstanding for their attractiveness and the Kitchen Mixer is no exception. The metal stand is of light green while the fluted glass mixing bowls, juice extractor and motor case are of French Ivory. All metal parts including the separable paddles are chromium plated. Each Kitchen Mixer comes complete with a large and small mixing bowl, juice extractor, drink mixer paddle and recipe book. The motor has a jet black Bakelite handle which is fully insulated— a very important feature.

MB 3019 Kitchen Mixer

$25.90

All prices subject to change without notice

MANNING-BOWMAN ELECTRIC APPLIANCES

UNIVERSAL KITCHEN HELPER

Experience has proved that many so-called electrical labor-saving devices are labor saving in name only. More time and energy are consumed in assembling and adjusting them than is saved by their operation. There are many kitchen tasks that are done more easily, more quickly and more simply by hand operated appliances... there are other tasks that are best done by motor driven devices.

The ideal appliance for each task, both electrical and hand operated is now combined in one complete unit—the new UNIVERSAL Kitchen Helper. It is easy to operate and easy to clean. No difficult assembly or adjustments complicate its uses—no glass to break—no danger of burnt out motors. It is the most practical combination of kitchen conveniences ever desired.

An attachment for every use and not a single complicated adjustment.

All attachments fit the same stand. Rigid, Powerful.

JUICE EXTRACTOR

VEGETABLE SLICER AND SHREDDER

FOOD AND MEAT CHOPPER

UNIVERSAL ELECTRIC

MIXING AND BEATING UNIT

POTATO RICER

COFFEE GRINDER

No. E796	Complete as illustrated	$37.60
No. E790	Consisting of Stand, Motor, Mixing Unit and two Bowls	22.60

Attachments for No. E790 Mixing Unit can be purchased separately as follows. The prices quoted do not include the stand shown in the illustrations.

No. 901	Juice Extractor	$2.70	No. 904	Potato Ricer	$1.70
No. 902	Food and Meat Chopper	2.70	No. 905	Coffee Grinder	4.10
No. 903	Vegetable Slicer and Shredder				4.70

In this new UNIVERSAL Kitchen Helper are found the famous features of the UNIVERSAL Mixer and Beater. Its tireless beaters help with hundreds of kitchen tasks. They beat eggs, mix batters, whip cream and mash potatoes. The entire beating unit may be carried to the stove to beat hot sauces or frostings. And in addition the base serves as a handy stand for those tried and tested attachments which, operated by hand have proved more efficient—more convenient.

Small bowl dia. 5½ in., capacity 1 qt. Large bowl dia. 9 in., capacity 3 qts. Unbreakable acid-resisting Porcelain Enameled Bowls, Ivory and Green decorations. Base has rubber feet. Large mixing bowl rests on revolving platform and is turned by the beating action on the batter—a feature that gives speed to mixing. Six foot rubber covered cord securely anchored and protected by coil spring which prevents kinking and strain at motor connection.

UNIVERSAL

PORTABLE
Beating unit may be used separate from stand.

SEPARATE BEATERS
Easily Removed
Easily Cleaned

THREE SPEEDS
A speed for every need operates on A. C. or D.C. current.

UNIVERSAL

Prices subject to change without notice.

THE MOST PRACTICAL MIXER WITH THE MOST SENSIBLE ATTACHMENTS EVER DEVISED TO LIGHTEN KITCHEN LABOR

Mixer Catalog Illustrations

POLAR CUB HOUSEHOLD MIXER

Ideal for mixing drinks, whipping cream, beating eggs, and all small household mixing uses.

Equipped with a standard Polar Cub Universal Motor,

Sold in 1930

110 volts, A. C. or D. C. cord and two-piece separable plug. Two-piece drawn steel shell, wood handle, and cast iron base finished in rubber enamel, black. Complete with cord and plug. Length over all handle and motor, 7$^{1/2}$ inch. Height over all is 9$^{5/8}$ inch. Base diameter is 6 inches. Complete weight is only 4 lbs. 6 ozs.

$65+

HAMILTON BEACH DRINK MIXERS

White enamel finish, automatic action, motor starts as cup slides into position,stops when cup is removed. Nickel silver cup. A sliding contact switch located in upright, motor operates on 105-120 volts A.C. 25-60 cycles or D.C. Complete with a 6ft. cord and plug.

Sold in 1928

$90+

ESKIMO KITCHEN MECHANIC

Ideal for mixing drinks, mayonnaise and dressings, whipping cream, etc. Finished in gray and white enamel, nickel trimmings. Operates on direct

Sold in 1928

or alternating 60 cycle current. Complete with adjustable stand, glass mixing bowl, 7 ft. of cord, toggle switch and plug.

$65+

HOME DRINK MIXER

For mixing drinks, beating eggs, whipping cream, etc. Can be used on the stand or in a bowl. High speed motor drives nickeled mixing arm. Complete with 5ft of cord and attaching plug. For any 105-120 volt current, draws 35 watts.

$65+

Sold in 1927

Mixer Catalog Illustrations

POLAR CUB BEATER

This mixer was made expressly for The Wesson Oil-Snowdrift People. It mixes mayonnaise and all light batters. Whips cream, beats eggs, etc. It does the job thoroughly and quickly. Its powerful motor and double intertwining agitator aerates evenly. Its standard rod is curved to enable the use of a large mixing bowl. The blades are easily detached for washing.

$70+

Sold in 1929

ESKIMO TWIN MIXER

This mixer will whip cream, beat eggs, mixes light batters or mayonnaise, in one-quarter the time of hand-worked. Aluminum cup for drinks, graduated 1-quart glass bowl, twin beater, and mixer. Finished in lettuce green enamel, nickel trimmings, adjustable stand and toggle switch.

$80+

Sold in 1931

KITCHEN MIXER

Mixes, beats eggs, mayonnaise, French dressing, malted milks and cool drinks. Finished in light green with nickel trimming. Equipped with stand holder, graduated mixing bowl, and extra whipping applicator. Toggle switch control.

Sold in 1931

$65+

DORMEYER CAKE MIXER

Mixes any food better, smoothly, quickly and evenly. Mashes potatoes and other vegetables, right in the kettle because it is not shackled to a stand. Beats eggs, mayonnaise, icing, whip cream, meringue, ice cream and mixes drinks. Four speed universal motor, with a hardened ivory finish and chromium plated mixing arms.

Sold in 1931

$50+

FRUIT JUICE EXTRACTOR

Strong dependable motor. Quickly takes the juice out of lemons, oranges or limes. White glass bowl, reamer and strainer are included.

$35+

Sold in 1933

51

Mixer Catalog Illustrations

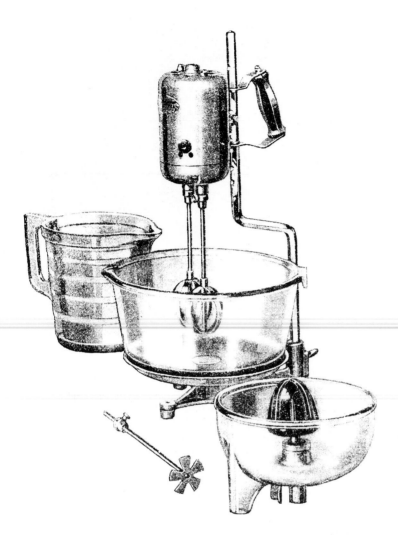

DORMEYER ELECTRIC FOOD MIXER & JUICE EXTRACTOR

Built sturdy and has adjustable stand equipped with revolving turntable and drink mixer beater. Finished in lustrous baked-on green enamel and has polished stainless steel beater blades. Universal motor, 110 volts, with a complete range of speeds. Includes one extra large mixing bowl and one 5 pint measuring pitcher which is graduated in pints, cups and ounces. Both made of clear crystal glass. The orange hued reamer, unbreakable and untarnishable beetleware.

$100+

GILBERT KITCHEN-ETTA

This is not only a beater and juice extractor but also an all purpose kitchen appliance. It does all kinds of beating and mixing, juice extracting, food chopping, drink mixing, coffee grinding, and an ice cube breaker. Fitted with double gear drive and an air cooled motor with four powerful outlets and three speed control variations for each function. This mixer includes bowls, cups, extractor, etc. Finished in ivory and is chromium plated.

$150+

Sold in 1932

Mixer Catalog Illustrations

Sold in 1933

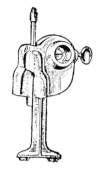

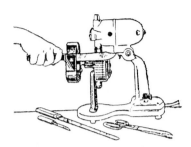

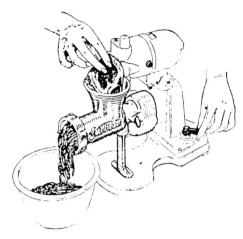

Power Transfer

$30+

Knife Sharpener Attachment

$50+

Food Chopper/Meat Grinder Attachment

$50+

SUNBEAM MIXMASTER POWER TRANSFER UNIT AND ATTACHMENTS

The **Power Transfer** can use any attachment for the Mixmaster. It is necessary to have a power transfer unit to reduce the speed and give corresponding increase in power. Designed for use with either Nos. 1, 2, M4F, M4H or M4J Mixmasters. One power unit is all that is necessary to use any of the attachment.

Knife Sharpener attachment will fit either Nos. 1, 2, M4F or M4H Mixmasters. Slip it in place of one of the beaters and must be used in connection with a power transfer unit which reduces the speed of the motor and gives the necessary smooth, sharp edge. Sharpens all kinds of knife blades and scissors.

The **Food Chopper and Meat Grinder attachements** will fit either Nos. 1, 2, M4F or M4H Mixmasters. Slip it in place of one of the beaters, must be used in connection with a power transfer unit. It cannot be stalled with the toughest meat or gristle, entirely enclosed power mechanism. Complete with food chopper, plate, coarse and fine vegetable cutters, meat grinding plate and meat knife.

ELECTRIC MIXER AND JUICE EXTRACTOR MIXMASTER

This Mixmaster can be stationary or portable, ivory enameled base with nickeled trimmings. Complete with two heavy green opaque glass mixing bowls and a juice extractor bowl with white porcelain reamer, adjustable oil dripper for making dressings, two beaters. This mixer can mix cakes, icing, batters, whip eggs, cream candy, mashed and whipped potatoes and other vegetables, extracting fruit juices. This can be used with all Mixmaster attachments.

$55+

Sold in 1934

WHIPMIX ELECTRIC MIXER

A heavy imitation onyx glass bowl 5" in diameter and 4¾" high, and the motor is enclosed in ivory baked enamel case with black wood knob on top for lifting from bowl. The opening in the cover permits adding ingredients while the motor is in operation and seeing the condition of mixture without removing the cover. Used for mixing icings, custards, whipping cream, beating eggs, etc. Complete with silk cord and plug.

$25+

Sold in 1934

53

Mixer Catalog Illustrations

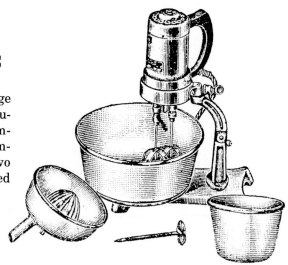

UNIVERSAL MIXER AND JUICE EXTRACTOR

Heavy cast iron base and bracket hinge finished in beautiful green enamel, die cast aluminum motor housing, nickel plated trimmings, two heavy Armco iron porcelain enameled mixing bowls and juice extractor, and two beaters. Lift from the stand and it may be used anywhere with any bowl or pan.

$115+

Sold in 1934

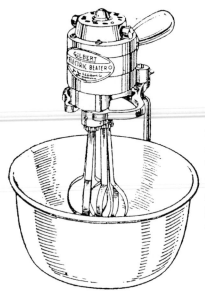

ELECTRIC EGG BEATERS

An enameled iron base and adjustable holder, finished in gray, nickel and blue, aluminum revolving mixing bowl. Standard can be turned so the blades of the agitator touch the inside of the bowl, when motor is started the bowl will revolve slowly if the contact on the inside of the bowl is light and more rapidly if the contact is increased. By turning the standard either to the right or the left the bowl revolves in either direction. The bowl is easily removed and a larger bowl substituted, complete with toggle switch and cord with a two-piece plug.

Sold in 1934 **$65+**

MONARCH WHIPPER

This Monarch will whip cream, beat eggs, and mix drinks. The whipping unit may be detached and used in any pan or bowl. Complete with glass bowl, and cord.

$25+

Sold in 1941

SUNKIST JUNIOR MIXER & JUICER

This famous Sunkist Jr. mixer combined with a newly designed and patented electric rotary cake mixer. Extracts fruit juices, beats and mixes batter, etc. Finished in chromium and verde green, extractor and mixer bowls are jade green glass.

Sold in 1934

$50+

54

Mixer Catalog Illustrations

G.E. HOTPOINT PORTABLE MIXER AND JUICER

This G.E. mixer is fully portable and may be used on the base or removed. Complete with double beaters, large and small Glasbake bowls, juicer, handy spatula and oil dropper and cord. Glasbake Juicer bowl has adjustable spout, cream colored porcelain reamer. The oil dropper is used for preparing salads. Many accessories will fit with this mixer, they are: drink mixing set, knife sharpener, grater, buffer, pea sheller and bean slicer, ice crusher, food chopper, slicer-shredder.

Sold in 1935   **$80+**

ELECTROMIX

A very useful household necessity consisting of glass bowl with high grade motor attached to cover. It has a detachable stainless beater which cleans instantly. The unit is portable and can be used anywhere. Complete with regulation cord and plug.

$40+

Sold in 1936

ELECTRIC WHIPPER AND MIXER

Complete with a bowl, motor, cord and plug. One pint glass jar with graduations. Stainless Steel mixer blade, and a portable electric unit for use anywhere.

Sold in 1937   **$35+**

ESKIMO MIXER-JUICER

Three speed motor, self cooling, all gears are sealed in grease. Complete with crystal glass juicer, two mixer bowls and a mayonnaise oil cup.

$115+

Sold in 1937

$90+

Sold in 1938

HOTPOINT MIXER

This multi-purpose mixer can extract juices, grates vegetables, cheese, mixes drinks, sharpens knives, polishes silverware and performs dozens of other tasks. Complete with two Glasbake bowls.

Mixer Catalog Illustrations

ELECTRIC WHIPPER

$25+

For whipping cream, eggs, sauces and drinks etc. Consists of a 24 ounce graduated glass bowl over which is fitted a speedy induction type motor enclosed in a green and white enameled case with a convenient curved handle, and a heavy durable beater which can also be used as a portable whipper in any pan or bowl.

Sold in 1939

K-M FOOD MIXER SET

Mixer has a powerful three speed motor controlled by finger tip adjustment, and two sturdy beaters. Highly chromium plated, motor head tilts for removing mixing bowls, turn table revolves automatically by mixing action of beaters.

Sold in 1939 **$75+**

MIXER

This mixer is for light mixtures such as whipping cream, beating eggs, mixing drinks etc. Black top stop handle and graduated quart pitcher. Motor and beaters are chromium plated.

Sold in 1939 **$25+**

QUICK-MIX-MIXER

Mixer that will beat eggs, whip cream, mix drinks, mayonnaise, custards and thin batters, with a stainless steel agitator, toggle switch and non-slipping grooved handle. Comes complete with an extra heavy graduated measuring glass with pouring lip, 1 quart size.

$45+

Sold in 1939

DRINK MIXER

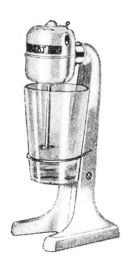

Sturdy home size mixer for malted milk or any other kind of drink. Complete with glass. In white enamel finish, and has a convenient toggle switch.

Sold in 1939 **$65+**

ESKIMO KITCHEN MECHANIC

This is more than just a drink mixer, it beats and whips also. Can be detached for stirring at the stove. Complete with a square molded-glass mixing bowl, for maximum mixing action. Cromium plated and walnut wood handles.

$75+

Sold in 1939

Mixers

STAR-RITE MAGIC MAID MIXER
 Model C, 105-115 volts, 70amps, 14¼" x 13½".
By The Fitzgerald Mfg. Co., Torrington, CT.

$65+

1941 SUNBEAM AUTOMATIC MIXMASTER
 Model 9, with extractor, 12¼" x 15", 110 volts,
120 watts. By Sunbeam Corp., Chicago, IL.

$45+

1939 HAMILTON BEACH MIXER & EXTRACTOR
 Model E, with two mixing bowls, 12"
x 16½", 115 volts, 120 watts. By Hamilton
Beach Co., Racine, WI, Division of Scovill
Mfg. Co.

$45+

1934 HAMILTON BEACH COMBINATION FOOD MIXER & EXTRACTOR
 Model B, with two mixing bowls,
12" x 16", 115 volts, 8 amps. By Hamilton
Beach Mfg. Co., Racine, WI.

$55+

Mixers

DORMEYER POWER-CHEF FOOD-FIXER

Model 4200, with two mixing bowls, the base is 12¼" L x 9" W x 12½" T, 115 volts, 150 watts.

$30+

1950's KENMORE MIXER

Model 303.82250, 120 watts. This Betty Crocker mixer was made for Sears, Roebuck & Co. which it also carries the brand name Kenmore. By General Mills Appliance Div. for Sears, Roebuck & Co., Mineapolis, MN.

$30+

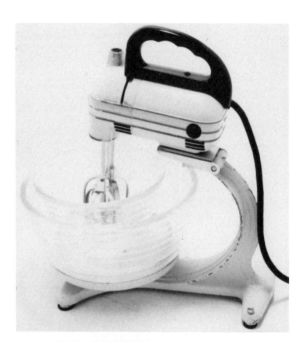

1937 G.E. MIXER

Metal mixer and base with black bakelite handle, cream color with green accent stripes and fluted glass bowls and juicer. Can be detached and used as a hand mixer. By General Electric.

$35+

1950's KITCHENMAID MIXER

Model 3-C, with a glass bowl, 1.2 amps. By Hobart Mfg. Co., Troy, OH. (The original model 3-A was patented in 1940).

$60+

Mixers

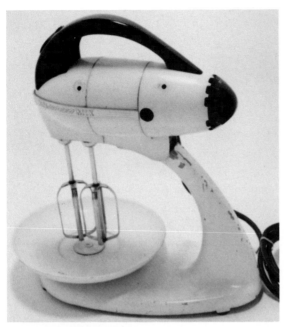

K-M SPEED MIX
Patented in 1942, 115 volts, 1.4 amps. By Knapp-Monarch, St. Louis, MO.

$30+

1946 MIXMASTER & COFFEE GRINDER
This common-easy to find mixer, has the coffee grinder attachment, the only one seen for years, 115 volts. By Sunbeam Corp., Chicago, IL.

$80+

HAMILTON BEACH MIXER
Model 51, drink mixer, 115 volts, 50 watts, 5" x 14½" x 7". By Hamilton Beach Co., Racine, WI, Made in U.S.A.

$50+

MIX-ALL MIXER "THE ELECTRIC BARTENDER"
Patented January 9, 1934, 110-120 volts, 4½" x 14" x 5". By Chronmaster Electric Corp., New York-Chicago.

$50+

Mixers

1934 HANDYWHIP MIXER

Another Handyhot Product, 105-115 volts, 50-60 cycle alt. current only. Made in the U.S.A., 4¼" dia. x 9½" tall. By Chicago Electric Mfg. Co., Chicago, IL.

$40+

CHALLENGER MIXER

Cat. No. 305-1146, 110-120 volts, 6 amps, 60 cyc. AC only, 4¾" dia. x 9¼" tall. By C.E.M. Co., made in U.S.A.

$25+

MECO MIXER

Cat. No. 4003, 110 volts, 60 c., 50 watts, 5" dia. x 7½" tall. By The Master Electric Co., Dayton, OH., U.S.A.

$25+

WHIPPER

Green depression glass bottom with wood handle on motor. The glass is marked "Vidrio Products Corp., No. E-20, Cicero, IL, Made in U.S.A.". The base is 3⅝" dia., the unit is 7⅛" tall.

$40+

WHIPPER

Chrome top with plastic handle, base is marked "Grand Sheet Metal Products Co., Home Appliance Divisions, Melrose Park, IL". Base is 4" dia., mixer is 9" tall.

$25+

1933 MODERNE MIXER

Cat. No. L-107, 60 cyc., 50 watts, 115 volts, AC only, 5" dia. x 8" tall. By Knapp Monarch Co., St. Louis, U.S.

$25+

Popcorn Popper Catalog Illustrations

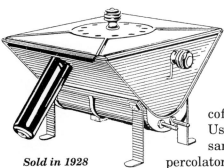

ELECTRIC CORN POPPERS

Sold in 1928

Pops corn, roasts coffee, peanuts, etc. Used on the table the same as a toaster or percolator. It has a crank for keeping contents in motion. Equipped with standard connections. Any standard iron or heater cord will fit. Capacity is 3 pints of popped corn, 30 watts.

$65+

CORN POPPER

Connects to any 105 to 120 volt light socket. Pops one-half gallons of corn in about five minutes. May also be used to cook bacon, eggs, chops, etc. Blue steel finish, 6 inches high, 8¼ inches in diameter. Complete with 6ft. of cord and attachment plug.

$25+

Sold in 1928

ELECTRIC CORN POPPER

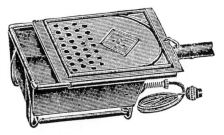

A 9 x 7 x 4 sheet metal popper. 13 inch tubular handle. 600 watts, nichrome heating element at bottom, with cord and plugs.

Sold in 1928

$40+

ELECTRIC CORN POPPER

Sold in 1931

$30+

Plugs into any 110 to 120 volt light socket or wall plug. Guaranteed heating element. Pops about half a gallon in five minutes. Made of polished blue steel.

ELECTRIC POPPER

Sold in 1933

Pops about 1/2 gallon of pop corn at a time. Long life with nichrome heating element. Plugs into a 110-120 volt current.

$25+

ELECTRIC CORN POPPER

Popper has a full nickel body, black handles, and a patented whip arm that prevents burning.

Sold in 1928

$20+

CORN POPPER

This popper has bright fittings, perforated top, 660 watt, and a nichrome heating element. The size is 6" high x 8½" in diameter.

Sold in 1934

$25+

KWIKWAY CORN POPPER

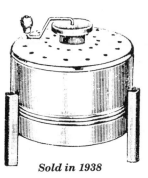

Sold in 1938

Makes fluffy, delicious popcorn quickly, half-gallon capacity. All steel construction, finished overall in bright aluminum baked enamel. Especially designed hinged lid with holes in top for shaking out unpopped kernels.

$30+

Popcorn Popper Catalog Illustrations

Sold in 1938

ELECTRIC CORN POPPER

Chromium plated, the side and agitator handles finished in walnut. Not furnished with cord but so constructed that any standard appliance cord may be used.

$25+

K-M TEL-A-MATIC CORN POPPER

This popper is thoroughly automatic in that it requires no shaking, no stirring, and no agitating the corn, when popped it is deliciously "buttered". Made of heavy aluminum, highly finished, with cool walnut handles, and a clear baking glass top, complete with Underwriters' Laboratories labeled cord.

Sold in 1938

$30+

U.S. POPCORN POPPER

Made of 25 gauge full finished steel with perforated top. Heating element is made from the highest quality of nichrome steel wire with extra heavy steel heat plate extending upward. Three red enameled wooden side holders or feet, handled and crank the handles.

Sold in 1939

$30+

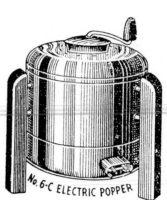

No. 6-C ELECTRIC POPPER

Sold in 1938

U.S. POPCORN POPPER

Constructed with seamless steel popping pan and side wall, highly polished chromium finish. Nichrome wire heating element with heavy heat plate extending upward, preventing butter from leaking through to heat element. Three blue enameled wooden handles or feet and crank.

$30+

Sold in 1940

TEL-O-MATIC CORN POPPER

Completely automatic corn popper that requires no shaking, stirring, or twisting or turning of an agitator. Corn is popped and buttered all in the same operation. Complete with a heavy glass cover that permits you to watch the corn as it pops.

$30+

JOLLY TIME CORN POPPER

Model 11, wood handle and legs, patented 1936, 110-120 volts, 475 watts, 7" dia. x 9" tall. By American Popcorn Co., Sioux City, Iowa.

$30+

Popcorn Poppers

DEPENDABLE DOMINO DEVICES POPCORN POPPER

Style No. 75, chrome with bakelite handles, 110-120 volts, 500 watts, 7¼" diameter and 9" tall. By Dominion Electrical Mfg. Co., Minneapolis, MN.

$30+

MINI POPCORN POPPER

Catalog No. 300, 115 volts, 140 watts, 5¾" x 8¼" x 10" with handle. By Rapaport Bros., Inc., Chicago, IL U.S.A.

$20+

1947 U.S. ELECTRIC POPPER

Catalog No. 10, with removable popping pan, 110-120 volts, 400 watts, 7¾" diameter x 9" tall. By U.S. Manufacturing Corp., Decatur, IL U.S.A.

$40+

K-M ELECTRICAL CORN POPPER

Aluminum with brown bakelite handles, 450 watts. By Knapp-Monarch Co., St. Louis, MO.

$30+

Early 1918 Hotpoint Items

Table Stove

Stove Catalog Illustrations

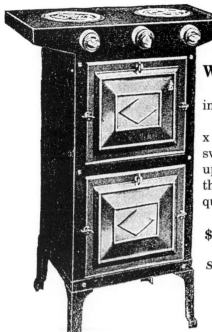

WHITE CROSS ELECTRIC CABINET RANGE

This range bakes, broils, boils, fries and roasts, that gives three different heating ranges up to 400°F, that does everything any electric range can do.

A full size range, 34 inches high, 14 inches wide, 12 inches deep. The top is 12 x 22 inches, with two burners operating independently with rotary "on and off" switch at each burner. Oven with reciprocating switch gives three different heats up to 400°F. Oven size is 12 x 10 x 11 inches. Same size warming closet. Made of the best grade of heavy pressed steel, double walled, asbestos lined, White Cross quality throughout.

$225+

Sold in 1930

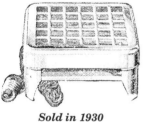

ALL-MUR STOVE

The highest grade of construction, element is made from nichrome, 110 volts only.

$15+

Sold in 1930

BLACK BEAUTY HEAVY DUTY STOVE

This is a large, sturdy electric stove, made strong to withstand work that is too heavy for the lighter stoves. Black finish, nichrome heating element inserted in grooved base. Furnished with cord and 2-piece plug.

Sold in 1930

$25+

Sold in 1930   **$35+**

WHITE CROSS STOVE

Each burner has individual switch. Nichrome element inserted in grooved insulated base, heavy black enamel finish, nickel trim – 110 volt only. Complete with cord and two piece plug. Draws 5.5 amp.

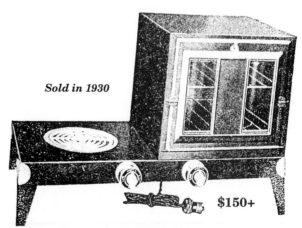

Sold in 1930

$150+

WHITE CROSS RANGE

These ranges are unusually substantial. Oven can be removed when not in use. Two burners with individual controls, heavy black enamel finish. 24 inches long, 11 inches wide, 5$^{1/2}$ inches high. Oven is 11 x 11 x 12 inches. Complete with cord and two-piece plug.

Stove Catalog Illustrations

UNIVERSAL TABLE STOVE

This stove broils, stews, fries, toasts and poaches. Frame and base is nickel plated. Pure aluminum pans. The stove has a deep pan or reflector cover, broiler grid and poacher rack with four removable cups. Equipped with a 6ft. heater cord, 660 watts.

Sold in 1928

$65+

THERMAX TOASTER STOVE

This toaster stove is made of steel, nickel plated. Top dimensions are $4^{5/8}$ x $7^{5/8}$ inches. Equipped with a 6ft. heater cord, 550 watts.

Sold in 1928

$20+

UNIVERSAL TABLE STOVE

This stove combines the advantages of a grill, toaster, chafer, fry pan and double boiler all in one. Cover and base are nickel plated. Cooking pans, egg poacher and cups are made of pure aluminum, highly polished. Cooking top is $6^{3/4}$ inch square. It has three degrees of heat, 160, 350, 650 watts. Equipped with a 6ft. heater cord and three heat indicating switches.

Sold in 1928

$75+

Sold in 1920   **$20+**

REDDY TOASTER RANGE

This range is 8 x $4^{3/4}$ inches, height is $2^{2/3}$ inches, nickel plated white sanitary legs, polished nickel shelf, keeps food warm, acts as an insulator. Boils, toasts, fries. To be used on 110 volts alternating or direct current, complete 6ft. extension cord.

PORTABLE STOVE

This portable stove or disc heater work for nursery, invalid's room, on the table and in other places. They are made in two styles, one without a switch and one with a three-point regulating switch, by means of which the heat can be controlled to meet the requirements. These stoves are all mounted on enameled slate bases, and operate equally well on direct and alternating currents on 110 volts. The stoves or any other devices fitted with a heat regulating switch have the double advantage of controlling the amount of heat and at the same time saving in cost of electricity.

Sold in 1920

$25+

Stove Catalog Illustrations

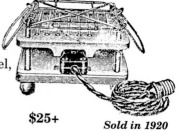

HOLD-HEET TOASTER STOVE

Sold in 1920

This stove is 110 volts 6 x 6 inches, 2¼ inches high, durable red asbestos composition, no metal, boils, toasts, and fries with direct or alternating current. Complete with a 6ft cord.

$20+

RED TOP TOASTER STOVE

Nickel plated steel, wire top, 110 volts, chromium resistance wire, nickel plated base, and hard wood ball feet. Operates for direct or alternating current. Complete with a 6ft. cord and socket.

$25+   *Sold in 1920*

Sold in 1920

PORTABLE RANGE

Nickel plated, especially adapted for use in kitchenette apartments, broils, fries, toasts, bakes or roasts, complete with 6ft. cord.

$75+

AMERICAN BEAUTY UTILITY STOVE

110 volts, top is 5 x 5, 3⅝ inches, sliding reflector plate made entirely of sheet steel, heavily nickel plated and polished. Complete with a 6ft. cord and attachment plug.

$20+   *Sold in 1920*

Sold in 1920

UNIVERSAL DISC STOVE

This 6 inch diameter disc stove, polished plate, two temperatures. Nickel plated frame, complete with a 6ft mercerized cord and ebonized handles and feet.

$25+

3 HEAT STOVE

Cooking surface of stove is 7 x 7 inches, switch attached, aluminum steel pans, boils, broils, steams, bakes, fries, conserves food, cooks your meals on the table. Complete with 6ft. of heater cord and connecting plug. For 110 volts direct or alternating.

$75+

Sold in 1920

UNIVERSAL DISC STOVE

Blued finish with nickel plated base and an ebonized handle. Twin connectors, 6ft. heater cord and separable lamp socket plug.

Sold in 1926

$25+

Stove Catalog Illustrations

Sold in 1921

$75+

ELECTRIC TABLE STOVE

This stove broils steaks, bacon, ham or pork chops. Boils, steams, fries or toasts. Bakes biscuits, muffins and cup cakes. Finished in polished nickel plate. Three pans are furnished, and broiler rack, cups and cup rack. Each pan is 7¾ inches square and they are ½ inch, 1¼ inch and 1¾ inch deep. The three heat switch permits the use of full, medium or low heat. Complete with a 6ft. cord.

$75+

Sold in 1922

ELECTRIC TABLE STOVE

Clean uniform heat is distributed over a 7 x 7 inch surface. This is the most convenient way to prepare bacon, steak and other meats, bakes muffins, biscuits, potatoes or cookies, steams rice, breakfast foods, custards, boils coffee, toasts four slices of bread at one time, with an assortment of aluminum pans including cup cake pans. Uses 660 watts on high, 330 on medium and 165 on low.

Sold in 1922

DUPLEX ELECTRIC KITCHENETTE STOVE

Cooks or toasts several foods at the same time. Especially convenient for preparing breakfast, light meals or lunch. Ideal for the nursery. Uses only 660 watts, or if only using one burner 330 watts.

$30+

COMBINATION TOASTER RANGE

Sturdy electric stove, makes toast, two slices at a time, grills meat, cooks, fries and boils without heating up room. Top size 9 x 5⅛ inches. Metal parts nickel plated and polished. Complete with a 6ft. cord and a plug. Uses 550 watts current.

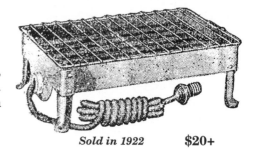

Sold in 1922 $20+

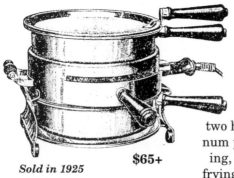

Sold in 1925 $65+

ROUND TABLE STOVE

Consists of two heavy aluminum pans for boiling, broiling or frying. Toaster, egg poacher and reflector cover, nickel plated. The stove is made with a double unit, three kinds of food can be prepared at one time. You can poach eggs on top, toast in the center and broil bacon or steaks in bottom.

HOTPOINT DISC STOVE

Made from pressed steel with cast iron top, polished nickel finish, moulded feet. Bottom shelf protects table or furniture from heat. Heat controlled by indicating snap switch. Cord attached to switch.

Sold in 1926

$25+

Stove Catalog Illustrations

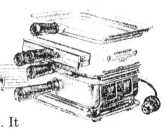

$65+

ARMSTRONG TABLE STOVE

Sold in 1926

This table stove can have three distinct cooking operations at the same time. It toasts both sides of the bread at once which doesn't interfere with other cooking operations such as broils, boils, toasts, fries, poaches, and steams. Complete with an egg-poaching attachment with four egg cups and all cooking utensils including, a waffle iron.

Sold in 1926

$20+

TABLE STOVES HOTPOINT

This stove has 36 sq. inches of cooking surface. It can toast, boil and fry. Removable top easily cleaned. The finish is highly polished nickel, fibre feet, both element and plug are removable.

HOTPOINT RADIANT STOVE

Sold in 1926
$25+

This stove cooks, toasts, and fries using ordinary utensils. Nickel plated steel throughout. Steel reflector under coil unit and a removable top for cleaning.

DISC STOVE

This is made of pressed steel with cast iron top, polished nickel finish, moulded feet. Bottom shelf protects table or furniture from heat. Cord with lamp socket and connecting plug.

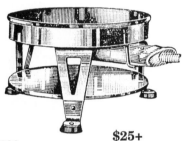

Sold in 1926

$25+

BLUE LINE TOASTER STOVE

Toasts two slices of bread, practical for light cooking. Nickel plated, 5¼ x 11½ inches, with 5ft of cord and a plug.

Sold in 1927

$20+

ELECTRIC CABINET RANGE

This stove has two plug receptacles, one for cooking on top burners, the other for oven baking. The two top burners are single heat, the oven is controlled by a three heat switch for low, medium, and high heat. The stove is 34 inches high, 14 inches wide and 12 inches deep. The oven has two heating elements. Made of sheet steel, satin finish, nichrome heating elements.

Sold in 1927

$225+

Sold in 1927
$35+

$20+

BLUE LINE DOUBLE BURNER TABLE STOVE

This durable stove has a cast base in silver brushed finish. The heating elements are constructed of nichrome wire. Complete with 7ft of cord and plug.

BLUE LINE SINGLE BURNER TABLE STOVE

This stove has three heat: low, medium, and high all controlled by one switch. It is 7¾ x 7¾ x 4 inches.

Stove Catalog Illustrations

STOVE AND OVEN SET

This three heat stove switches from low, medium and high. Oven is made of blue steel, lined with sheet metal and interlined with asbestos. Two baking racks and a clear glass window. Complete with 5½ ft. of cord and attaching plug.

$125+

Sold in 1927

TABLE STOVE

Nickel plated, asbestos protector under heating element. Complete with 6ft cord and equipped with separable attachment plug. 110 volts, 550 watts, 6¼ x 5¼ inches.

$20+

Sold in 1927

$150+

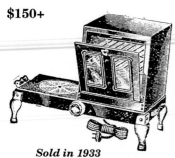

Sold in 1933

ELECTRIC OVEN TYPE STOVE

Black finish, nickel legs. Two burners, nichrome element. A three heat switch, (1120 watts) one side for baking only. Gives 550 watts on one side and 600 watts on the other side.

ELECTRIC TABLE STOVE

A practical stove that can be used to cook a whole meal right at the table. It fries, boils, toasts, bakes, and steams. All aluminum rustproof construction, three heat reciprocating switch. Comes supplied with two deep pans, one roasting rack, four cups for poaching eggs or muffins and deflector pan.

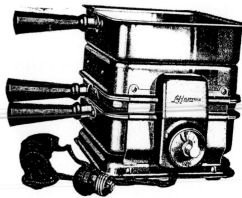

Sold in 1933

$75+

STOVE/GRILL

This new model table stove or grill is finished in metalescent gray, black and chromium, and one piece steel body mounted on four ebony finished wooden legs. It has an asbestos lined reflector base, and individual switches for each burner, and jewel light indicates when heat is on.

$35+

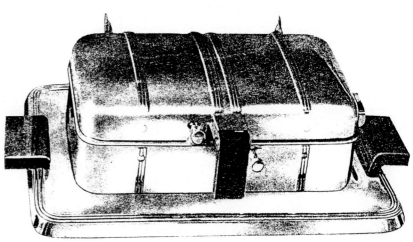

Sold in 1939   **$25+**

TABLE COOKER

This cooker bakes, broils, grills, toasts, and fries. Toasts two large sandwiches, fries bacon and eggs, broils steaks, etc. Bakes golden waffles too by means of the interchangeable waffle grids. Chromium finish, walnut mounts. A grease drain and pan included.

Stoves

BREAKFASTER
Aluminum with black bakelite handles, 115 volts, 750 watts. Hotplate on top – open the door to use as a toaster oven or bun warmer. By Caulkin Appliance Co., Niles, MI.
$65+

UNIVERSAL MULTI BREAKFAST COOKER
No. E788, 110-120 volts, 660 watts, pat. march 7, 1922. (Makes toast, poached eggs, and bacon or hash browns, etc.), 9" x 11¼" x 9". By Landers, Frary and Clark, New Britain, Conn. U.S.A.
$75+

Early 1918 Hotpoint Items

Toaster – $25+

Toaster – $40+

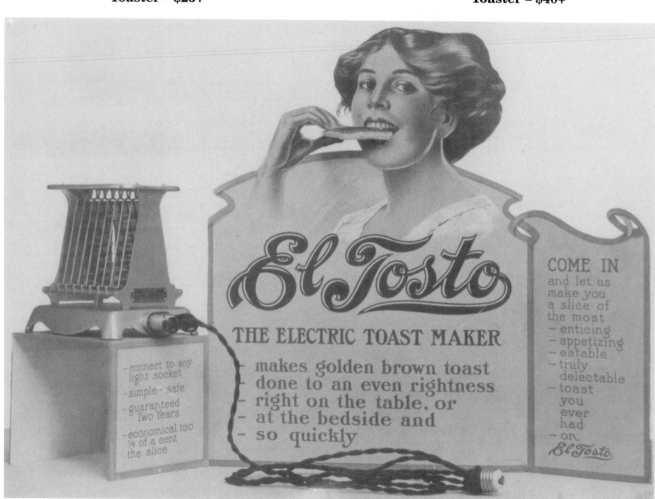

Toaster only – $85+

Toaster Catalog Illustrations

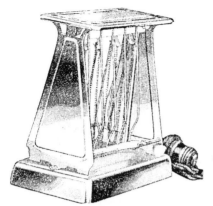

Sold in 1930

$25+

LIBERTY FLOPPER TOASTER

Two slice upright toaster, nickel plated. 7¼ inches high, 7¼ inches wide and 9 inches deep.

Comes complete with a 6 ft. cord and two-piece plug.

DeLUXE GOLD SEAL TOASTER $40+

Mirror nickel finish, genuine nichrome element, wired complete, with cord and plug, 110 volts. 7 inches high, 6½ inches long, and 3½ inches wide.

Sold in 1930

MARION GIANT "FLIP FLOP" TOASTER

This two slice toaster has toast turning doors, insulated handles. The element is made of the best resistance wire laced on clear mica. All parts are coppered, heavily nickeled and highly polished.

Sold in 1930   **$30+**

DOUBLE THORO-BREAD TOASTER

Toasts both sides of the bread at the same time. The elements are completely covered making them last longer and the big feature is that the toasting is done with applied heat instead of driven heat making the toast moist, not dried and crispy. It also came in a Single Thoro-Bread Toaster.

Sold in 1930

$45+

STAR-RITE REVERSIBLE TOASTER

Turns the bread without touching. Heavily nickel plated. Complete with cord and plug, 110 volts.

$45+

Sold in 1930

SUNBEAM ELECTRIC TOASTER AND TABLE STOVE

Sold in 1930

Toaster turns the bread over and toasts it flat. Toasts any sandwich of any shape or thickness. A wide variety of tasty dishes can be quickly prepared with the Sunbeam. 6¾ inches wide, 10 inches long, and 4⅛ inches high. Comes complete with a 6½ ft. cord.

$50+

Toaster Catalog Illustrations

UNIVERSAL SPRING CLAMP TOASTER

Nickel plated, one slice toaster, 5½ x 4½ inches. Equipped with 6 ft. art silk heater cord, 550 watt.

Sold in 1928

$25+

UNIVERSAL TURNEASY

$25+

Turns one slice of toast by simply turning the bread rack outward with the thumb and finger. Steel and nickel plated. 5½ x 5¼ inches. Equipped with a 6 ft. art silk heater cord, 625 watts.

Sold in 1928

UNIVERSAL OVEN TYPE

$65+

Push button switch in cord, steel nickel plated, sliding bread rack. Takes a slice of bread 4½ x 6 inch. Equipped with a 6ft. art silk heater cord, 550 watts.

Sold in 1928

UNIVERSAL REVERSIBLE TYPE

Swinging bread rack opens like a door, steel nickel plated. Takes a slice of bread, 4 x 4½ inches. Equipped with 6ft. art silk heater cord, 350 watts.

$40+

Sold in 1928

THERMAX SPRING CLAMP TOASTER

Toaster is steel, nickel plated. Toasts a slice of bread 4½ x 4½ inches. Equipped with a 6ft. heater cord, 400 watts.

Sold in 1928

$25+

THERMAX TURN EASY TOASTER

Toaster is steel, nickel plated. Toasts a slice of bread 5½ x 5¼ inches. Turns the toast by turning the bread rack outward with thumb and fingers. Equipped with a 6ft. heater cord, 550 watts.

Sold in 1928

$25+

L. & H. TOASTER DAMPER DOOR TYPE

This toaster is extra large, steel, nickel plated both inside and out. Takes a slice of bread 4¾ x 5¾ inches. Toaster has a bread reversing turnsit type mechanism in one piece. Equipped with a 7ft. heater cord, 500 watts.

Sold in 1928

$25+

TURNSIT TOASTER

Extra large toaster, steel, nickel plated inside and out. Takes a slice of bread 4¾ x 5¾ inches. Toast is reversed every time the door is dropped. Equipped with a 7ft. heater cord with feed-through switch, 550 watts.

$25+

Sold in 1928

Toaster Catalog Illustrations

Sold in 1918

ELECTRIC TOASTER

The electric heater is set on black enameled base, balance nickel plated. On each side is a door which swings outward and down opening sufficiently to permit placing or removing bread without burning the fingers. The toast rack on top increases the capacity by providing a place to keep the toast hot while other toast is being made or for drying out the toast in advance.

$75+

ELECTRIC TOASTER

Nickle plated, complete with cord and lamp socket.

Sold in 1918

$30+

FLIP FLOP TOASTER

Toaster is 110 volts, 5 x 7 x 6³⁄₄ inches highly nickeled, cold rolled steel block, ebony feet. Complete with a 6ft. cord, control switch on the cord and attachment plug.

$25+

HOLD-HEET TOASTER

Nickel plated, 110 volts, toasts two slices of bread at one time. Toast holders are spring operated, complete with a 5ft. cord.

Sold in 1920

$25+

TOASTER

A two slice, 6³⁄₄ inch, nickel plated toaster. Pressed steel throughout, with an elaborate design. Top rack can keep it warm, strong spring, with a 6ft. cord.

Sold in 1920

$25+

TOASTER

Toaster is 6³⁄₄ inches, two slices, nickel plated, fiber feet, with a 6ft. cord. Strong spring holds bread firmly in place.

$25+

Sold in 1920

Toaster Catalog Illustrations

TOASTER

Toaster is nickel plated, black enamel base, toasts two slices at once. Complete with 6ft of cord.

Sold in 1920

$30+

REVERSIBLE DOOR TOASTER

Toaster is nickel plated, with black enamel base. When one side of bread is toasted, turn the knob and the toast automatically turns over. Complete with 6ft. of cord.

Sold in 1920 **$40+**

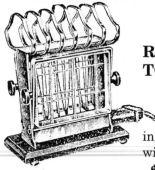

REVERSIBLE DOOR TOASTER

Toaster and base is nickel plated, with a rack on top for keeping the toast warm, complete with a 6ft. cord.

$75+

Sold in 1920

SIMPLEX TOASTER

Toaster is nickel plated steel, solid spring doors, complete with quick releasing connector, 6ft. cord and lamp socket plug.

$25+ *Sold in 1920*

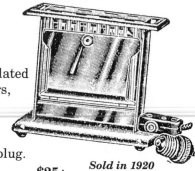

AMERICAN BEAUTY TOASTER

Toaster is 7 inches high, 8 inches in length, and 4 inches in width. Sheet steel, removable heating element, nickel finish. Complete with a 6ft. cord, plugs and lamp socket attachment plug.

Sold in 1920

$25+

FLAT TOP TOASTER

Convenient electric toaster and stove for home use. Make toast quickly. Liquids can be heated, and has many other uses. Operates on 105 to 115 volts. Heating surface is 5 x 5½ inches.

Sold in 1921

$20+

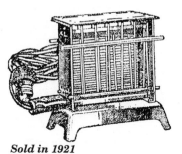

ELECTRIC TOASTER

Nickel plated toaster. Toasts two slices of bread at one time. Furnished with 5½ ft. of cord and plug for connecting. Suitable for use on all 105 to 115 volt circuits.

Sold in 1921

$25+

UNIVERSAL ELECTRIC TOASTER

Toaster is nickel plated brass base and stand, fiborite feet, removable perforated top plate, nickel plated wire heating guards, nickel plated spring toast holders, patent steel heating element coiled around three sections of mica. Complete with six feet of silk covered insulated cord and Hubbell lamp socket plug.

Sold in 1922

$25+

Toaster Catalog Illustrations

UNIVERSAL REVERSIBLE TOASTER

Nickel plated brass base and stand, easy swinging bread holder, cool fibre handles and feet, patent heating element. Complete with six feet mercerized cord and lamp socket plug.

Sold in 1921

$45+

UNIVERSAL TOASTER

Nickel plated frame, fibre feet, toast rack, comes complete with 6ft of silk cord and separable socket plug.

$75+

Sold in 1926

HOTPOINT REVERSIBLE TOASTER

Toasts two slices of bread and is not necessary to touch the bread until both sides are fully toasted. Steel nickel plated finish, cool fibre handles and feet, comes complete with cord and plug.

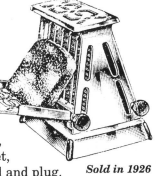

Sold in 1926

$25+

TWIN OVEN TOASTER

Toasts both sides of two slices of bread at the same time and much faster than the ordinary type of toaster. Heavily nickel plated, $6^{1/2}$ x 7 x 7 inches. Complete with 6ft of cord and attachment plug. For any 105-120 volt current.

Sold in 1927

$50+

BLUE LINE TOASTER

Toasts two slices at one time. Pulling down shield automatically turns toast, browns evenly. Nickel plated, highly polished. $7^{3/4}$ x $6^{1/4}$ x 8 inches. Complete with about 6ft. of cord and plug.

Sold in 1927

$25+

ELECTRIC TOASTER

Nickel plated, nichrome wire heating element, black enameled feet and knobs, 7 x 7 x $4^{3/4}$ inches, 110 volts. Complete with 6ft black cord with separable plug.

$25+

Sold in 1927

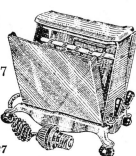

ELECTRIC TOASTER

Nickel plated, nichrome wire heating element, porcelain insulated fiber feet, 7 x 7 x 4 inches. Complete with 6ft of super heater cord and separable attachment plug and detachable contact plug.

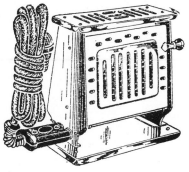

$25+   *Sold in 1927*

ARISTOCRAT LIBERTY TOASTER

Nickeled and polished, two doors with Tuscan Rosewood knobs and handles with nickel brackets and convenient off and on switch for table control.

Sold in 1929

$25+

Toaster Catalog Illustrations

HOTPOINT "TOGGLE TOASTER"

It gets its name from the convenient toggle switch that turns the toaster on and off without removing the plug. It is a toastover type, beautiful in design and finish, correctly built to produce perfect toast, and moderately priced.

Polished, nickel plated steel, cool metal handles, toggle switch in base, detachable miniature plug, non-scratching fiber feet, open coil heating unit, cord and plug.

Sold in 1928 $25+

TOASTMASTER

Toasts automatically without watching or turning. Drop the bread into the slot and press down the two levers, the toast will pop up automatically when finished.

Sold in 1929 $35+

UNIVERSAL ELECTRIC TOASTER DE LUXE

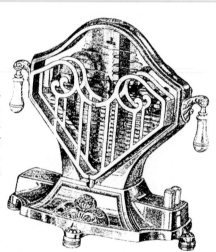

Original both in shape and design. The bread is turned by simply pressing ivoroy knob on base. Ivoroy pendant handles, decorated base, heavily nickel plated on brass. Complete with a push-through switch in cord.

$275+ *Sold in 1929*

MARION FLIP FLOP TOASTER

Toasts 5½ x 6 inch slices of bread rapidly and you turn toast without touching the bread. Heavily nickel plated.

$25+

Sold in 1929

HOMELECTRIC TOASTER

This toaster has a 600 watt element which will toast bread quickly, gives an even toast. Highly nickel plated finish.

Sold in 1928 $25+

Toaster Catalog Illustrations

TIP-AND-TURN TOASTER

Tip the door all the way open and the bread turns over, ready to toast the other side. Made of brass, finished in nickel and ornamented with a chased design.

Sold in 1928

$25+

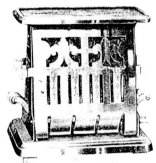

OLD ENGLISH PATTERN TOASTER

Turn-easy type chromium plate blue diamond finish, ivory antique casein handles, knobs and feet. Push button switch attachment plug. $25+

Sold in 1929

GE HOTPOINT TOASTER

Drop bread in, set the handy click and its done, without watching. Toasts both sides at once. Shuts off current automatically. Hot plate chromium finish, calmold base, die-chased paneled sides, cool handles on sides.

Sold in 1931

$60+

Sold in 1931 $50+

TRUE BLUE LINE TOASTER

Toaster with an automatic timer, two slices are done in a few seconds. Sparkling non-tarnishing chromium finish wipes bright with a cloth. An 8 x 8 x $10^{3/8}$ inches overall.

Sold in 1931

BLUE LINE SANDWICH TOASTERS

Grills, bakes, toasts, fries etc. Also comes with waffle grids, and ever cool handles. The left one is sparkling chromium plated finish, the right one is highly polished nickel-plated finish.

$35+

Toaster Catalog Illustrations

OVEN TOASTER

This oven toasts both sides of the slices at the same time. Nickel-plated finish. Complete with cord and plug.

$45+

Sold in 1931

BLUE LINE WARD'S FINEST TOASTER

This flip-flop toaster has a sparkling chromium finish that will not tarnish, easy to clean. Toasts two slices at a time. Automatically turns toast when door is pulled down. Westinghouse patented.

Sold in 1931
$30+

FLIP-FLOP TOASTER

This Westinghouse patented flip-flop toaster is nickel plated, toasts two slices at the same time and automatically turns toast when door is pulled down.

$25+ *Sold in 1931*

TOASTER

This serviceable toaster is very low priced. A polished nickel finish and nichrome mica element with two green carrying handles on the sides. A rayon cord and push plug.

$25+

Sold in 1931

HOMELECTRIC TOASTER

This 600 watt element toaster gives a very even toast. Heavily nickel plated.

$25+

Sold in 1931

MANNING-BOWMAN TIP AND TURN TOASTER

This Westinghouse patented flip-flop toaster is nickel plated, toasts two slices at the same time and automatically turns toast when door is pulled down.

$25+ *Sold in 1931*

Toaster Catalog Illustrations

TOASTWATCH TOASTER

The "Toast-watch" Toaster is equipped with a clock work mechanism that acts automatically in shutting off the current before the toast can burn and toasts two slices of bread at once.

$25+

Sold in 1931

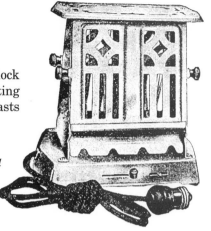

MANNING-BOWMAN TIP & TURN TOASTER

Nickel plated, 600 watt element with lava bushing protection. Turns the toast and made the best ever.

$25+

Sold in 1920

Sold in 1932　　**$75+**

ELECTRO AUTOMATIC TOASTER

Toasts two slices of bread at one time and automatically ejecting the toast when finished. Chromium plate and emphasized with contrasting color trim. Measures 6" x 8½ x 6, equipped with a crumb drawer for easy cleaning.

TORRID TURNOVER TOASTER

Nichrome ribbon element on pure mica core insures an evenly distributed heat. Built rugged for lasting service. Toast two slices of bread at the same time, finished in chromium plate.

$25+

Sold in 1932

Toaster Catalog Illustrations

STAR-RITE TOASTER

An automatic switch that can be set for any degree of toasting, and shuts off itself. The enclosed oven type casting keeps toast hot even after it shuts off. Chrome finish with engraved panels. Toasts two slices at one time.

Sold in 1932

$35+

TOAST-MASTER TOASTER

This one slice toaster toasts both sides at the same time. Operates automatically, ejecting the toast when ready to

$35+

Sold in 1932 serve. Finished in highly polished chromium plate on heavy metal blanks.

TOAST-MASTER TOASTER

This two slice toaster toasts both sides at the same time. Operates automatically, ejecting the toast when ready to

$40+

Sold in 1932 serve. Finished in highly polished chromium plate on heavy metal blanks.

MARION GIANT TOASTER

Highly polished, chromium plate flip-flop toaster . Operating the gates turns the toast. All parts are made of copper and nickel-plated. Will take two large slices of bread.

$30+   *Sold in 1932*

DOUBLE ACTION TOASTER

Toasts two full slices of bread on both sides at the same time, and each side is exactly as you want them. A heavy nickel finish and black handles. Complete with cord and plug.

$60+   *Sold in 1932*

TOAST-O-MATIC

Set to any desired degree. Beautifully finished in highly polished chrome. Stands 8⅝" high and base is 11¾" x 5½". Comes com-

Sold in 1932 plete with switch, plug and cord.

$100+

Toaster Catalog Illustrations

SLICE TOASTER

Turns all four pieces of toast with one movement of the lever. No sticking or jamming. Highly nickel plated. Equipped with nichrome heating element, full length cord, plug and off-and-on switch.

$125+

Sold in 1932

SANDWICH TOASTER

Built durably of the best materials and finished in brilliant nickel plate. Toasts both sides at the same time, and is equipped with dependable heating element, adjustable cover to admit different thickness of bread and everything that

Sold in 1932   **$30+**

can be reasonably expected of a first class appliance.

HANDYHOT ELECTRIC TOASTER

Toasts two slices of bread at the same time on both sides of the slice. Its efficiency is due to the oven type construction. Equipped with quick heating element of 500 watts capacity. Complete with cord and plug. **$40+**

Sold in 1932

"SPEE DEE" SPECIAL

Sturdy and efficient toaster, makes evenly crisp toast in the shortest possible time.

Brightly nickeled, equipped with attachment

$55+   *Sold in 1932*   cord and plug. Will

toast two sides of bread at same time.

2-SLICE TOASTER

Finished in chromium plate, bakelite fittings. Uniform toasting without watching. Just set the lever for degree of browness you desire. Cord and plug included.

$35+

Sold in 1933

BREAD OR ROLL TOASTER

Special expansion hinge permits the toasting of bread, rolls and muffins. Bakelite crumb tray with handles which permits moving toaster while hot. **$25+**

Sold in 1933

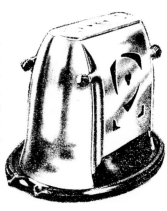

FOSTORIA SANDWICH TOASTER

Finished in chrome plate, with handles of walnut bakelite. Long-life heating elements in the base and cover. Toasts two sandwiches at once, it is also a convenient grill for table use. Complete with matching spatula.

$35+

Sold in 1940

FOSTORIA FOURSLICE TOASTER

This lustrous chrome plate finished toaster with walnut bakelite handles toasts 4 slices of bread at the same time. Has an extra large nichrome heating element and a tray base to catch the crumbs. The doors turn toast automatically when opened.

$50+

Sold in 1940

83

Toaster Catalog Illustrations

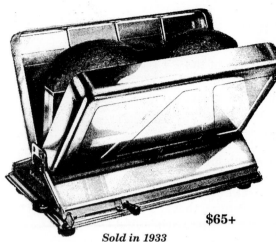

EDICRAFT TOASTER

Automatic two slice toaster that toasts both sides at once. When toasting is completed it does not turn off the current, but removes the heating from the toast to prevent burning and continues to keep the toast warm until used. Oven type construction, with bakelite handles and feet.

$65+

Sold in 1933

MONARCH TOASTER

Sold in 1934

A complete sandwich toaster, bread toaster, grill, frying pan and hot-plate, finished in highly polished nickel plate, ebonized handles, special adjustable hinge allows top grid to be placed at desired height for making sandwiches of different thicknesses, 6" steel grids with grease rings which prevent grease overflow, fibre feet, and an imbedded type element.

$45+

Sold in 1941

TEL-A-MATIC TOASTER

Entirely automatic, no preheating. Just set the dial for light to dark toast, switch shuts off when toast is done. Complete with a mica element, chrome case, and cord. **$35+**

ESTATE TOASTER

Nickel plated throughout the base, frame and top. Four pieces of bread can be toasted at one time. Bread can be turned without touching with your hands. The switch in connecting cord controls the current at all time. Complete with standard cord and two piece plug.

Sold in 1934

$125+

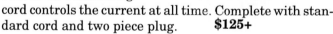

GEORGE WASH-INGTON TOASTER

Toasts two slices of bread at one time. Opening the bread rack turns the toast. Made of the best materials, nickel plated, fibre handles and feet, hand laced mica element, no cord or plug furnished. **$55+**

Sold in 1934

STAR-RITE TOASTER

Double reversible two slice model, copper shell, nickel plated and engraved with bakelite handles and turning knobs, heating element uniformly distributed. Complete with a variegated silk thread cord with detachable plug and two piece attachment plug, 115 volts.

Sold in 1934

$45+

Toaster Catalog Illustrations

UNIVERSAL TOASTER, EMPIRE PATTERN

Toasts two slices of bread at the same time on both sides. Set the lever and the bread will automatically be delivered entirely free from the oven when it is toasted, although the current will remain on continuously. Chromium plated, bakelite knobs and fibre feet. 10⅝" tall and equipped with a 6 feet of art silk cord with plug and push button switch.

$100+

Sold in 1934

FLAT TOASTER SUNBEAM

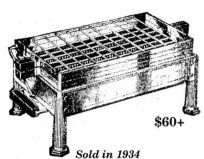

$60+

Sold in 1934

The Sunbeam flat toaster also uses the principal of rising heat which makes it toast faster. An adjustable hinge permits rack to accommodate slices of any thickness, even two full sandwiches at a time.

SUNBEAM TOASTWITCH

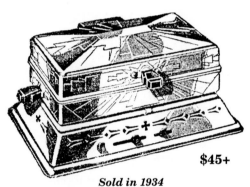

$45+

Sold in 1934

Toasts faster because it uses the principle of rising heat and is particularly desirable for it toasts slices of any thickness and sandwiches lie flat, so filling won't fall out. When toast is done, cover pops open, heat is shut off and wire fingers raise the toast off of the elements. Chromium plated with etched design.

Sold in 1934   **$30+**

DE LUXE ELECTRIC TOASTER

Finished in chrome and jet black. Makes two large slices of toast at the same time. Mica-core heating element assures evenly browned toast. Complete with non-scratching fibre feet and a long detachable cord.

TOASTER

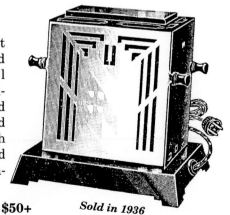

Toasts two slices at same time. With hard baked black enamel finish and highly polished nickel finished doors. Black wood knobs attached to both doors and supplied complete with regulation cord and plug.

$50+   *Sold in 1936*

STREAMLINE ELECTRIC TOASTER

This toaster has a mica element and is the turn over type with chromium doors, top and panels. Ebony black frame and base. Bakelite feet and handles.

$150+

Sold in 1937

Toaster Catalog Illustrations

BERSTED'S FOUR SLICE TOASTER

Rich black and chrome finish, cool bakelite handles, nichrome mica heating element. 6¾" x 12".

$40+

Sold in 1937

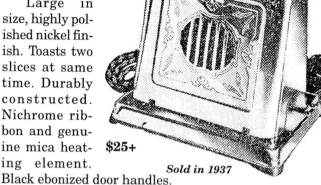

TOASTER

Large in size, highly polished nickel finish. Toasts two slices at same time. Durably constructed. Nichrome ribbon and genuine mica heating element. Black ebonized door handles.

$25+

Sold in 1937

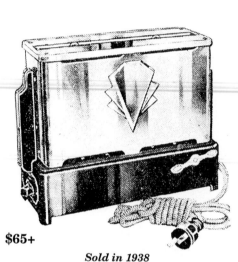

$65+

Sold in 1938

K-M ELECTRIC TOASTER

This toaster is 8¼" high and the base is 4" x 10" made of black bakelite. The top and sides are highly polished chromium plate. The clock device is on the end, and rack raiser lever is in front. One pull of the switch for light toast, two for medium and three for dark. A signal bell rings when toast is ready.

Sold in 1938

$20+

TEL-A-MATIC ELECTRIC TOASTER

This toaster with its streamline design, polished chromium plate with walnut handles, toasts bread evenly every time. The lever at the side permits any shade of toast – light or dark. The signal cuts off the current when toast is done.

Sold in 1938

"JUNIOR" TOASTER

This toaster is not fully automatic, but it has many outstanding features. Just press down the lever and the current comes on. When the toast is done, a finger touch of the lever pops it up, both sides browned at once.

$20+

TOASTMASTER

A fully automatic two slice toaster, modern in style, finished in chromium. The base, handles and other moulded parts are dark brown bakelite, with a permanently attached cord and unbreakable rubber plug to match.

$40+

Sold in 1938

Toaster Catalog Illustrations

SAMSON TRIMATIC TOASTER

$150+

Toasts three slices of bread at the same time. This toaster can be converted from one slice toaster to a three slice toaster by merely turning the switch. Heat unit wound on mica to assure even baked toast. All of the sturdy

Sold in 1938

mechanism is built in the bakelite base away from the heating chamber, and it keeps the clock mechanism cool and requires no oiling.

K-M TEL-A-MATIC TOASTER

Sold in 1938 $65+

This toaster maintains constant control without watching. One setting of toast shade control is all that is necessary. The end panels open for convenient cleaning. Toast carrier is controlled by ornamental red knob. All handles are of genuine walnut, heating element is made of nichrome.

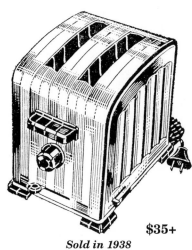

SON-CHIEF TOASTER

This two slice toaster is automatic, toasts two slices of bread at the same time evenly because of proportioned body. Paneled and finished in sparkling chrome plate, with black bakelite handles, feet and knobs and a mica

$35+

Sold in 1938

unit with ribbon wire element.

SUNBEAM TOASTER

Toasts two slices of bread or two sandwiches at one time. Patented hinges expand to admit sandwiches of any thickness or thin crackers, rolls, etc. Can be used as a table stove by

$60+

Sold in 1939

tipping back the toasting rack or removing it completely. Finished in Chromium plate with handles made of black bakelite, complete with 6ft. cord and plug.

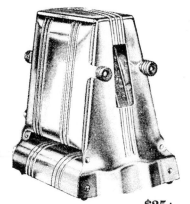

VIZ-O-LITE TOASTER

A modern designed toaster with two outstanding features, the turn-o-matic feature where the two doors are lever-linked, by lowering one side both doors open simultaneously and both slices of toast are turned at the same time. Viz-O-Lite feature is a light inside the toaster that en-

$25+

Sold in 1939

ables you to see through an opening at the end to see how the bread is toasting. Chromium plated finish, with black handles.

TILT-TOASTER

Equipped with patented button which releases top so that it can be tilted or lifted from base for easy cleaning or removing

$30+

Sold in 1939

crumbs. Toast turns automatically as doors are lowered. Chromium plated finish with walnut handles.

Toaster Catalog Illustrations

TOASTER

Polished chromium plated finish toaster with bakelite handles, black base. Toasts two slices of bread in two minutes.

Sold in 1939   **$25+**

TIME CONTROL TOASTER

This popular Airline design is a two slice turn-over toaster. Chromium plate and black enamel inlay. Set the heat indicator for the kind of toast you want and the bell rings when the toast is ready.

Sold in 1939   **$25+**

AUTO-FLIP TOASTER

Chevron design toaster in sparkling chromium plate and ebony colored finish. Toast turns automatically as doors are lowered.

$20+   *Sold in 1939*

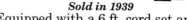

EXPAN-DOR TOASTER

Embossed side panel doors, expanding hinge control of doors permits sandwich toasting. Finished in chromeplate with black handles.

Sold in 1939
Equipped with a 6 ft. cord set and plug.   **$25+**

$55+   *Sold in 1939*   **$75+**

TWO SLICE TOASTER   FOUR SLICE TOASTER

These two Toastwell Toasters are automatic and equipped with a Time Master Control. A bell rings when the toast is done, and the toaster automatically reverts to low heat, keeping the toast hot until ready to serve. This low heat feature makes it possible to make melba toast.

Toaster Catalog Illustrations

No. KE401 – UNIVERSAL TOASTER

Has a nichrome wire wound on thick mica core that assures fast and even toasting. The rack swings down at finger's touch. The current shuts off automatically. Complete with black bakelite handles and feet and a 6ft. cord and push botton switch.

Sold in 1940

$60+

Sold in 1940 **$50+**

No. KE402 – BELL SIGNAL TOASTER

The bell rings when the toast is ready and switches the current from a toasting heat to a low serving heat. Ideal for making "Melba" toast. Complete with a nichrome wire wound on thick mica core that assures fast and even toasting. Complete with handles and feet chromium plated.

Sold in 1940

No. KE403 – DOUBLE QUICK OVEN TOASTER

This toaster makes delicious oven toast at the table, two slices at a time. Toast rack tilts forward at the touch of a finger. Has a nichrome wire wound on thick mica core. Finished in chromium with black bakelite handles and fibre feet. **$60+**

No. KE404 – DEVONSHIRE PATTERN MUFFIN AND BREAD TOASTER

This charming motif of this pattern is taken from the Adam design which was so popular during the early 18th Century. Mahogany

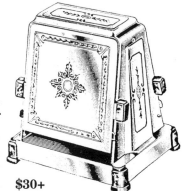

$30+

Sold in 1940

composition trim, with a specially designed bread rack that also holds muffins. Chromium plated with a nichrome wire wound on thick mica core that assures fast and even toasting.

Sold in 1933

No. 563D1863 – TOASTER/GRILL

Toasting sandwiches is not the only thing this appliance can do. The top folds back and makes a double surface grill for cooking bacon and eggs – pancakes or hamburgers. The grills are 8½" long by 5³⁄₈" wide.

$35+

No. GE4473 – TOAST-O-LATOR

The only home toaster that keeps the slices moving while they are being toasted. Completely automatic. Just put the bread in one end, the toast you ordered comes out the other end. The chromium shell is easily removed for cleaning, complete with black bakelite base.

$200+

Sold in 1940

Toasters

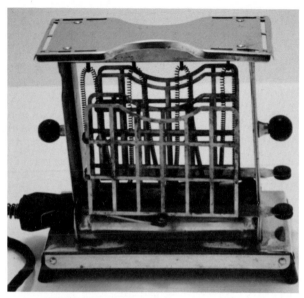

TORRID TOASTER
Stainless with wood handles, has swing-a-way bread slots, 110 volts, 5.7 amps, 8" x 7", patented February 15, 1927. By The Beardsley & Wolcott Mfg., Co., Waterburg, Conn.
$65+

1938 MODERN HOME SINGLE AUTOMATIC TOASTER
No. E1608-5, 110-120 volts, 450 watts, 7½" x 7". By Modern Home Appliance Co., Philadelphia, PA.
$20+

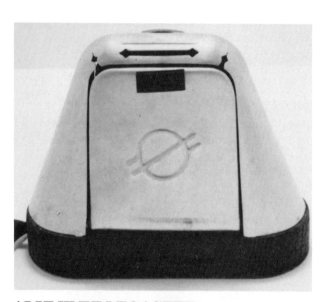

ALUMINUM TOASTER
A product of Riverside Mfg., Co., Ypsilanti, MI, 7" x 9".   **$30+**

HOTPOINT TOASTER
Chrome with wood handles, cata. no. 125T22, patented July 23, 1914, 110 volts, 550 watts, 7¼" x 7¼". By Edison Electric Appliance Co., Inc.
$25+

Toasters

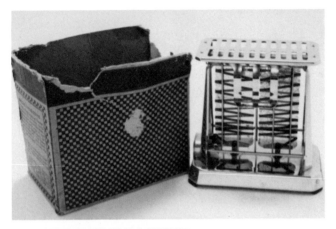

MINI CHILD SIZE TOASTER
110 volts, 150 watts, 43/4" x 4". By Excel Electric Co., Muncie, Ind. U.S.A.
$40+

HOTPOINT TOASTER
Chrome, cat. no. 114T5, 32 volts, 450 watts, 6¹⁄₂" x 7". By Edison Electric Appliance Co., Inc., NY, Chicago, Ontario, Cal.
$70+

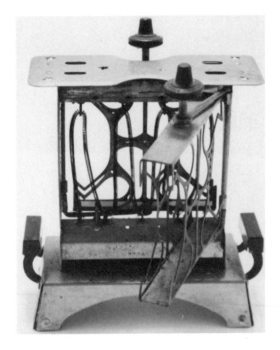

STAR ELECTRIC TOASTER
Metal with plastic handles, has swing-a-way bread slots, 115 volts, 550 watts, 7¹⁄₂" x 8". By Fitzgerald Mfg., Co., Torrington, Conn.
$45+

Toasters

MESCO

Chrome with wood handles and porcelain base, 110 volts, 450 watts with a swing out bread slot, 8" x 8½". By Manhattan Electrical Supply, mid 1910's.

$150+

ROYAL ROCHESTER SINGLE SLICE TOASTER

Chrome with plastic handles, 110-120 volts, 465 watts, 7¼" x 8". By Robeson Rochester Corp., Rochester, NY.

$25+

UNIVERSAL TOASTER

Stainless, No. E941, 110 volts, 3.1 amps, 6½" x 7¾". Oct. 5, 1915, by Landers, Frary & Clark, New Britain, Conn. U.S.A.

$25+

TURNOVER TOASTER

Model A-2332, Serial #231570, 110 volts, 5.7 amps, 6½" x 7". By Westinghouse Electric & Mfg. Co., East Pittsburgh, PA.

$25+

Toasters

WESTINGHOUSE TURNOVER TOASTER

    Catalog #TTC-114, chrome with wood knobs, 7" x 7¼", 115 volts, 500 watts. By Westinghouse Elec. & Man. Company, Mansfield Works Mansfield, Ohio, U.S.A.

      $25+   *(also pictured on page 94)*

SON-CHIEF TURNOVER TOASTER

    Series 680, 5½" x 7¼" x 9¼", 550 watts, 115 volts. By Son-Chief Electrics, Inc., Winsted, Conn. U.S.A.

      $20+

DOMINION SINGLE SLICE TOASTER

    Chrome with wood handles and feet, style #1104, 7¼" x 7½", 110-120 volts, 450 watts. By Dominion Electrical Mfg., Inc., Mansfield, OH.

      $25+

1926 L & H ELECTRIC TOASTER

    Two slice toaster, nickel plated, black bakelite handle, 550 watts. By The A. J. Lindemann and Hoverson Co., Milwaukee, WI.

      $55+

Toasters

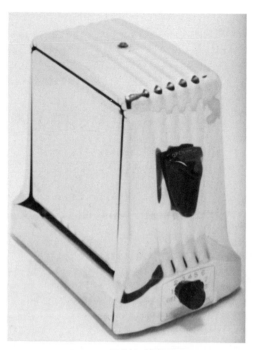

G.E. HOTPOINT TOASTER

Catalog #129T41, two slice, chrome with black bakelite handles, 950 watts. Both doors open when knob is rotated. This is the only "clamshell" toaster I know of that has heating elements in the doors — browning both sides of the bread at once. It also has a browness selector, indicator light, and bell to signal that toast is done, art deco design. Advertised in 1935, by General Electric, Bridgeport, CT.

$65+

UNIVERSAL TOASTER

Two slice, chrome, with brown bakelite handle, 500 watts. (Turn handle to lower both doors). By Landers, Frary & Clark, New Britain, CT.

$45+

DOMINION TOASTER

Two slice, chrome with black bakelite handles, style #1109, 450 watts. By Dominion Electric Manufacturing Inc., Mansfield, OH.

$45+

WESTINGHOUSE TURNOVER TOASTER

Patented 7-28-14, 8-25-15, 115 volts, 500 watts, 5½" x 7" x 7¼". By Westinghouse Elec. & Mfg., Co., Mansfield Works, Mansfield, Ohio, U.S.A.

$25+ *(also pictured on page 93)*

Toasters

WESTINGHOUSE TOASTER
Two slice, chrome with wood handles and base, 500 watts. By Westinghouse, Mansfield, OH.

$40+

G.E. HOTPOINT TURNOVER TOASTER
Catalog #159T25, 115 volts, 5" x 6¾" x 8". By General Electric Co., Bridgeport, Conn., Ontario, Calif.

$25+

DEPENDABLE DOMINO DEVICES TURNOVER TOASTER
Style 49, 5¼" x 6½" x 7½", 110-120 volts, 500 watts. By Dominion Electrical Mfg., Co., Minneapolis, Minn.

$35+

SON-CHIEF TOASTER
Single slice toaster, chrome with wood handles, series 680, 115 volts, 550 watts, 7¼" x 9¼". By Son-Chief Electrics, Inc., Winsted, Conn.

$15+

Toasters

BERSTED TURNOVER TOASTER
Model 68, 8" x 7½" x 12", 115 volts, 400 watts.
By Bersted Mfg., Co., Fostoria, Ohio.
$20+

MIRACLE TOASTER
Chrome with bakelite handles, cat. no.
210, 115 volts, 400 watts, 6½" x 7". By Miracle
Electric Co., Chicago, IL, U.S.A.
$25+

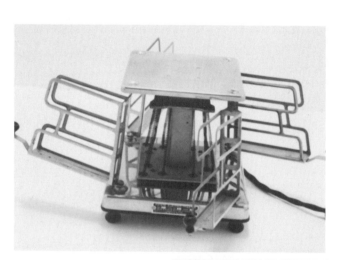

ESTATE ELECTRIC TOASTER
No. 177, chrome with bakelite switch on cord, 4 slice swing out style toaster. 110 volts, 5.5
amps, 7" square base, 5⅞" tall x 7" base. By The Estate Stove Co., Hamilton, Ohio.

(two views, the one on the left shows how the toaster opens up).
$125+

Toasters

WESTINGHOUSE TURNOVER TOASTER

Cat. #TEC-14, 5½" x 7 x 7½", 115 volts, 400 watts. By Westinghouse Elec. & Manufacturing Company, Mansfield Works, Mansfield, Ohio, U.S.A.

$25+

SPEED-MASTER TURNOVER TOASTER

Series 680, with wood handles, 5¾" w x 7¼" t x 12" l, 550 watts, 115 volts. By Son-Chief Electrics, Inc., Winsted, Conn. U.S.A.

$25+

CORONET TOASTER

Series 680, chrome with wood handles, 115 volts, 550 watts, 7½" h x 11½" l, also has a flip out bread slot. By Connecticut Appliance Co., Winsted Conn.

$25+

VOGUE PRODUCTS TURNOVER TOASTER

No. A305, 375 watts, 110 volts, 6" x 7½" x 8¾". By Sheridan Electro Corp., Chicago, U.S.A.

$25+

Toasters

TRIANGLE TOASTER STOVE
Cat. No. 3320, 3¼" tall x 6¾" dia., 95-109 volts, 550 watts. By Triangle Lektrik Sales Co., Detroit, MI.

$25+

O-KAY STOVE-TOP TOASTER
Patented 1924, 115 volts, 4 amps, 2¾" x 5¼" x 6". By O-Kay, Sandusky, Ohio.

$20+

RUTENBER ELECTRIC TOASTER
Model 205, chrome with wood handles, pat. Feb. 6, 1906, 115 volts, 660 watts, 4½" tall x 7" sq. By Rutenber Electric Co., Marion, IN.

$25+

GREAT NORTHERN TOASTER
Three slice toaster, chrome and black with plastic handles, 110-120 volts, 700 watts, 8½" x 8½" x 8½". By Union Metalworks Corp., Unionville, Conn., manufactured for Great Northern Products Co. **$100+**

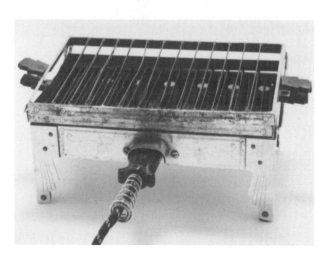

SUNBEAM TOASTER
No. 4, unique deco design chrome and with bakelite handles, 120 volts, 660 watts, 4½" high x 10½" wide. **$60+**

Toasters

1936 KWIK*WAY TURNOVER TOASTER
Cat. No. 21-404, 5½" x 7½" x 8¼", 115 volts, 400 watts. By Kwik Way Co., St. Louis, U.S.A.
$25+

FOSTORIA TOASTER
Single slice toaster, chrome with plastic handles, model #72, 115 volts, 400 watts, 7½" x 10". By Bersted Mfg. Co., Fostoria, OH.
$25+

1939 STERLING TOASTER
Single slice toaster, chrome and black with wood handles, cat. no. 5804, 7½" x 8", 115 volts, 400 watts. By Chicago Electric Mfg., Co., Made in U.S.A.
$25+

1930 KNAPP MONARCH TOASTER
Stainless, cat. no. 250, 110 volts, 550 watts, 6½" tall x 6¾" high. By Knapp Monarch Company, Webster City, Iowa.
$25+

Toasters

ROYAL ROCHESTER TOASTER
Stainless with plastic handles, cat. no. 13400, 120 volts, 500 watts. Toaster has a bell type timer, 6½" x 6½". By Robeson Rochester Corp., Rochester, NY.

$20+

TOASTMASTER TOASTER
Two slice toaster, chrome with brown bakelite handles, 7" x 10½", 115 volts, 9.5 amps. By McGraw Electric Co., Toastmaster Products Div., Minneapolis, MN.

$20+

1945 UNIVERSAL TOASTER
Two slice toaster, chrome and bakelite, model #EA-B2601, 7¾" x 8¾", 110-120 volts, 1150 watts. By Landers, Frary & Clark, New Britain, Conn.

$20+

GENERAL ELECTRIC TOASTER
Two slice toaster, catalog #129181, 7½" x 12". Chrome with brown bakelite, 115 volts, 1150 watts. By General Electric Co., Bridgeport, Conn.

$20+

Toasters

1946 WESTINGHOUSE TOASTER
Chrome with black bakelite handle, cat. no. TO-91, 7¼" x 11", 115 volts, 1000 watts. By Westinghouse, Mansfield, OH.
$30+

1950 SUNBEAM TOASTER
Two slice toaster, chrome with black bakelite handles, model T-20, 7½" x 11½", 110-120 volts, 1275 watts. By Sunbeam Corp., Chicago, U.S.A./Toronto, Canada.
$20+

CONTROLA TOASTER
A child's toaster, (heats up very slowly), tin, 3¾" x 5¾".
$35+

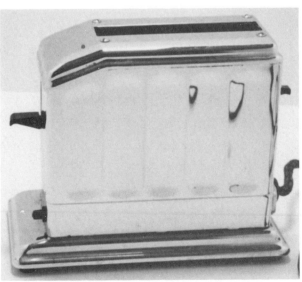

1928 TOASTMASTER TOASTER
One slice toaster, chrome with plastic handles, model 1A2, 110 volts, 600 watts, 7¼" x 9". By Waters-Genter Co., Minneapolis, MN.
$35+

1942 SUNBEAM TOASTER
Model T-9, chrome and plastic with jewel, made in the U.S.A., 7¾" x 10". By Chicago Flexible Shaft Co., Chicago, IL.
$45+

Toasters

UNIVERSAL TOASTER
No. E7822, chrome with bakelite handles, 120 volts, 660 watts, 7¼" x 7½". By Landers, Frary & Clark, New Britain, Conn. **$60+**

1941 TOASTMASTER TOASTER
Automatic pop-up, two slice toaster, chrome with brown bakelite handles, 110-120 volts, 10 amp, model 1B12, 7¼" x 11". By McGraw Electric Co., Toastmaster Products Div., Elgin, IL.
$15+

1941 TOASTMASTER TOASTER
Model 1B14 automatic pop-up toaster, chrome with brown bakelite handles, two slice, 7½" x 11½", 110-120 volts, 10.5 amps. By Toastmaster Prod. Division, McGraw Electric Company, Elgin, IL.
$15+

Toasters

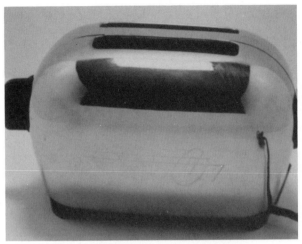

1945 TOASTSWELL TOASTER
Two slice toaster, chrome with black bakelite, No. 996, 110-120 volts, 920 watts, 7" x 12". By The Toastswell Co., St. Louis, MO.
$50+

1945 GENERAL ELECTRIC TOASTER
Two slice toaster, chrome with brown bakelite handles, cat. no. 159T77, 115 volts, 1150 watts, 7½" x 11½". By General Electric Co., Bridgeport, Conn./Ontario, Calif.
$15+

WESTBEND TOASTER
Model 3232E, chrome with black handles, series 6201, 110-120 volts, 1050 watts, 7¼" x 11". By The West Bend Company, West Bend, WI.
$15+

GENERAL ELECTRIC TOASTER
Two slice toaster, cat. no. 129T81, chrome with brown bakelite, 7¼" x 12", 115 volts, 1150 watts. By General Electric Co., Bridgeport, Conn.
$15+

Toasters

GENERAL ELECTRIC TOASTER
Two slice toaster, chrome with black bakelite handles and feet, cat. no. 82T82, 115 volts, 1150 watts, 7¼" x 11½". By General Electric Co., Brideport, Conn.   **$15+**

1939 TOASTMASTER TOASTER
One slice toaster, chrome with brown bakelite handles and base, model #1A5, 110 volts, 650 watts, 7" x 10¼". By McGraw Electric Co., Toastmaster Products Div., Elgin, IL.
$15+

1945 WESTINGHOUSE TOASTER
Two slice toaster, chrome with brown bakelite handles and base, cat. no. TO-501, 7¼" x 10", 115 volts, 1320 watts. By Westinghouse, Mansfield, OH.
$15+

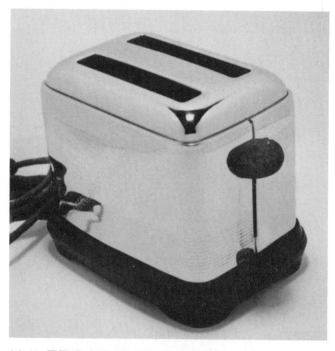

1945 PROCTOR TOASTER
Model 1466A, two slice, chrome with brown bakelite handles and base, 100 watts. By Proctor Electric Co., Philadelphia, PA.
$35+

Toasters

DOMINION TOASTER
    Two slice, not automatic, style #1105, chrome with wood handles, 660 watts. By Dominion Electrical Manufacturing Inc., Mansfield, OH.
$20+

1939 WESTINGHOUSE TOASTER
    Two slice chrome toaster with brown bakelite handles and base, cat. no. TK-14, 1100 watts. By Westinghouse, Mansfield, OH.
$35+

1947 GENERAL MILLS
    Automatic pop-up toaster, cat. no. GM5A, two slice, chrome, and black bakelite, 1200 watts. General Mills introduced their Betty Crocker appliances shortly after W.W.II. They sold out their appliance business 6 or 7 years later. By General Mills Appliance Division, Minneapolis, MN.
$30+

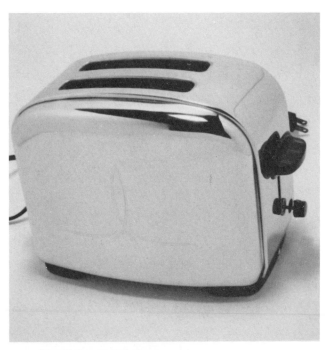

GENERAL DELUXE AUTOMATIC POP-UP TOASTER
    Two slice toaster, chrome with black bakelite handles, 950 watts.
$20+

Toasters

SPEED-O-MATIC TOASTER
Series 612, two slice, chrome and black bakelite toaster, 115 volts, 750 watts. By Son Chief Electric Inc., Winsted, Conn.
$30+

1938 G.E. TOASTER
Cat. No. 129T75, two slice toaster, chrome with black bakelite, 115 volts, 1100 watts. By G.E.
$30+

1939 HEATMASTER TOASTER
Model 360.6330, two slice, chrome toaster with black bakelite handles, 1100 watts. By Heatmaster.
$40+

SUPERSTAR TOASTRITE
Two slice, chrome toaster with wood handles, 575 watts. Unusual wood feet and art deco design embossed on sides.
$40+

Toasters

1942 K-M TOASTER

Two slice toaster, chrome with brown bakelite handles, 400 watts. To open toaster, clockwise rotation of handle opens one side of toaster. Counter clockwise turn of handle opens other side. By Knapp-Monarch, St. Louis, MO.
$45+

SAMSON TOASTER

Model 5147N, two slice, chrome toaster with brown bakelite base and knobs, 1100 watts. Place bread slices end to end. By Samson United Corp., Rochester, NY.
$55+

MID 1930'S TOASTWELL TOASTER

Two slice chrome toaster with black bakelite handles and feet, 630 watts. Nice art deco design, detachable cord, "Doneness" selector. By Utility Electric Co., St. Louis, MO.
$50+

HEETMASTER AUTOMATIC TOASTER

Model 360.2094, two slice, chrome toaster with black bakelite handles and feet, 1150 watts. Art deco handles and design engraved on sides and front.
$45+

Toasters

PENN-AIR "POP-DOWN" TOASTER

Model 280, two slice aluminum toaster with black bakelite handles, 940 watts. Penn Air went into the toaster business right after World War II to use up the aluminum allocations. Toast drops down into the chutes on both sides when toast is done, this toaster is very desirable for toaster collectors. By Pennsylvania Aircraft Works Inc., Philadelphia, PA.

$100+

DOMINION ELECTRIC TOASTER

Model 1115-C, two slice, chrome toaster with black bakelite handles and base, 660 watts. By Dominion Electric Corp., Mansfield, OH.

$25+

WARDS AUTOMATIC POP-UP TOASTER

Model 944VCG2291A, two slice, chrome with black bakelite handles and base, 1150 watts. Sold and marketed after WWII. A Camfield Toaster in Montgomery Ward disguise. By Camfield Manufacturing Co., for Montgomery Ward.

$25+

1939 K-M TOASTER

Two slice, chrome toaster, brown bakelite handles and base, 890 watts. By Knapp-Monarch, St. Louis, MO.

$40+

Toasters

KENMORE TOASTER

Model 344-6332, two slice, chrome toaster, red bakelite handles and base, (also seen in green, yellow and brown, 1200 watts. By Arvin (Noblitt-Sparks) Industries for Sears, Roebuck, Columbus, IN.

$35 for other colors $25 for brown

ROSEBUD TOASTER

Model 25-1, two slice, chrome, black bakelite handles and feet, 825 watts. By Radiron Corp., Miamisburg, OH.

$65+

1950 CAMFIELD "TET-A-TET" TOASTER

Model T24, two slice, chrome, with black bakelite handle/base, 10 amps. By Camfield Manufacturing Co., Grand Haven, MI.

$40+

1953 TOASTMASTER

Model 1C5, three slice, chrome toaster, with brown bakelite handles and base., 120 volts, 12 amps. By Toastmaster Division of McGraw Edison, Elgin, IL.

$20+

Toasters

1940 WESTINGHOUSE TOASTER
Two slice, chrome toaster, 115 volts, 1150 watts. By Westinghouse, Mansfield, Ohio.

$30+

1940 TOASTMASTER
Model 1B9, two slice, chrome toaster with brown bakelite handles. This toaster was introduced in the fall of 1939 with a full page color ad in Life Magazine.

$20+

1938 TOASTMASTER
Model 1B8, two slice, chrome toaster, brown bakelite, 120 volts. By McGraw Electric Co., Minneapolis, MN.

$30+

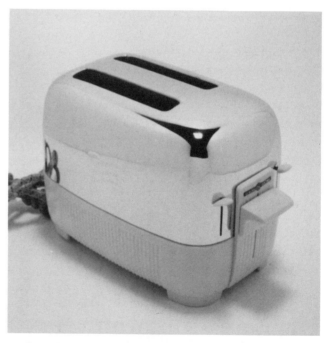

1951 G.E. TOASTER
Two slice, chrome with ivory bakelite handles and base, 115 volts, 1150 watts.

$30+

Toasters

1953 WESTINGHOUSE TOASTER

Two slice, chrome toaster with brown bakelite base, 115 volts, 1320 watts. By Westinghouse, Mansfield, Ohio.

$30+

HANDYHOT TOASTER

Type AEUB, chrome with black bakelite base and handles, 110 volts, 500 watts. Art deco design, very rare. By Chicago Electric Mfg. Co., Chicago, IL.

$150+

KENMORE AUTOMATIC POP-UP TOASTER

Two slice, chrome toaster with black bakelite handles, 115 volts, 1170 watts, 10.2 amps. Manf. date stamp 11-48. By Arvin (Noblitt-Sparks Industries), Columbus, IN.

$20+

1938 TOAST-O-LATOR

Model G, chrome with black bakelite base and handles, 600-850 watts. Toast moves through a walking conveyer. By Crocker-Wheeler Electric Mfg. Co., Ampere, NJ.

$200+

Toasters

MERIT MADE TOASTER

Model Z, two slice, chrome toaster with black bakelite handles and painted steel, 375 watts. By pulling the plunger up opens both sides. Some models you push plunger down to open doors. Two slice pop-up also came in this bodystyle. By Merit Made Inc., Buffalo, NY.

$75+

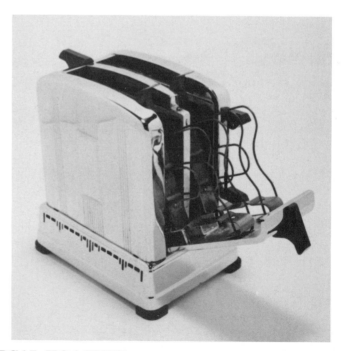

1937 UNIVERSAL TOASTER

Two slice, chrome toaster with black bakelite handles, 110 volts, 800 watts, series E7822A. Put bread in the top, door swings out when toast is done. By Landers, Frary & Clark, New Britain, Conn.

$60+

Toasters

1932 TOASTMASTER
One slice, chrome toaster with black bakelite handles, 110 volts. By McGraw Electric Co., Minneapolis, MN.
$35+

1932 TOASTMASTER
Two slice, chrome toaster with black bakelite handles, 115 volts. By McGraw Electric Co., Minneapolis, MN.
$35+

1944 DORMEYER
Model EA-6500, chrome with black handles, 115 volts, 1150 watts. (This toaster is identical to the Universal models EA-2815 & EA-B2601 except for the engraved side design.) By Landers, Frary & Clark.
$20+

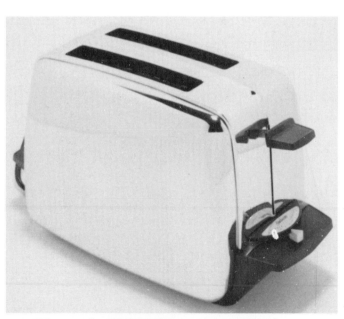

LATE 1940's SUNBEAM TOASTER
Two slice, chrome toaster with brown bakelite handles, 1150 watts. By Sunbeam, Chicago, IL.
$20+

Toasters

1936 SUNBEAM TOASTER
Model T-1C, two slice, chrome toaster with black bakelite handles and base, 875 watts. By Sunbeam, Chicago, IL.

$65+

1946 MONITOR
Model C28, two slice, chrome toaster with brown bakelite handles and feet, 8 amps. By Monitor Equipment Corp., New York, NY.

$20+

1956 WESTINGHOUSE TOASTER
Two slice, chrome toaster with black bakelite, 1320 watts. By Westinghouse, Mansfield, Ohio.

$20+

1936 K-M TEL-A-MATIC TOASTER
Two slice, chrome toaster, red bakelite & wood handles, 800 watts. This toaster is not automatic. The red bakelite knob raises and lowers toast. Unusual design for placing toast end to end. By Knapp-Monarch, St. Louis, MO.

$65+

Toasters

 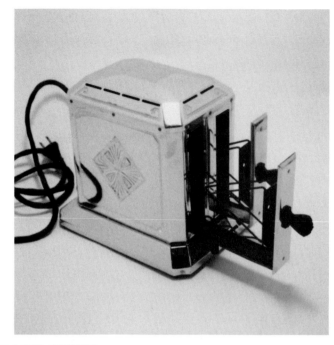

COLEMAN TOAST OVEN

Two slice, chrome toaster with black bakelite handles, 575 watts. Patented April 29, 1930. By Coleman Lamp & Store Co., Wichita, KS.   **$120+**

1938 TOASTWELL TOASTER

Two slice, chrome, with black bakelite handles and feet. Unusual art deco design on sides, 660 watts. By Utility Electric Co., St. Louis, MO.

$50+

1938 AUTOMATIC TOASTWELL

Four slice, chrome toaster with black bakelite handles and feet, 1100 watts. Unusual art deco design on sides. By Utility Electric Co., St. Louis, MO.

$70+

Toasters

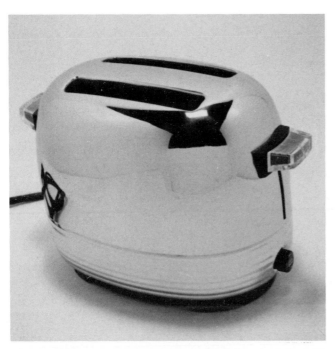

1951 PROCTOR AUTOMATIC POP-UP TOASTER

Model 1481, two slice, chrome toaster with black bakelite and clear plastic handles, 1000 watts. By Proctor Electric Co., Philadelphia, PA.

$45+

KNAPP-MONARCH TOASTER

Two slice, chrome toaster with brown bakelite handles and base, 1060 watts, advertised in 1949. By Knapp-Monarch, St. Louis, MO.

$35+

ARVIN TOASTER

Model 4000, two slice, chrome toaster with black bakelite, 1170 watts. 1941 patent, by Arvin "Noblitt-Sparks" Industries, Columbus, IN.

$35+

MERIT MADE TOASTER

Model A, two slice, chrome toaster with black bakelite handle, 800 watts. By Merit Made Inc., Buffalo, NY.

$65+

Toasters

CAMFIELD TOASTER

Model 24-1-2, two slice, chrome toaster with brown bakelite handles and base, 10 amps, patent 1944. By Camfield Manufacturing Co., Grand Haven, MI.
$35+

1947 KENMORE TOASTER

Model 874.63290, two slice, chrome toaster with black bakelite, 115 volts AC/DC, 10.5 amps. Toastmaster for Sears Roebuck & Co.
$25+

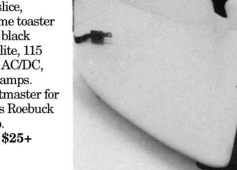

1938 SUNBEAM TOASTER

Model T-1-C, two slice, chrome toaster with black bakelite handles and base, 875 watts. By Chicago Flexible Shaft Co., Chicago, IL.
$45+

MAGI-CRAFT TOASTER

Model 677, two slice, chrome toaster with brown bakelite handles, 750 watts. By Son-Chief Electric Inc., Winsted, CT.
$35+

1944 UNIVERSAL TOASTER

Model EA-2815, two slice, chrome toaster, black bakelite handles, 1150 watts. The toaster has a servue feature, the lower part of the activator handle may be used to raise the bread while toasting to check on degree of browning. By Lauders, Frary & Clark.
$25+

Waffle Iron Catalog Illustrations

Sold in 1930

STAR-RITE WAFFLE IRON

Has two heating elements, one upper and one lower which makes waffles more quickly than any other iron on the market. A start and stop switch is supplied with the cord. Handle is self-balancing. 110 volts only.

$35+

BERSTED WAFFLE IRON

Nichrome heating elements on both sides – not necessary to turn waffle over. Heavily nickel plated, grids made of aluminum, slotted hinge allows for expansion, with black ebony handle. Equipped with 6 ft. cord and two piece plug. Iron is 7¼ inches in diameter, height overall is 6 inches, weight is 4¾lbs.

$20+   *Sold in 1930*

Sold in 1930

JIFFY ELECTRIC WAFFLE IRON

Makes a quick and good waffle. Made of the best material obtainable. The Jiffy represents the very highest development in waffle iron construction. Highly polished finish, compact and light.

$20+

GOLD SEAL WAFFLE IRON

A beautiful nickel plated Waffle Iron that is an ornament on any table. It has heating elements on top and bottom and is quality made throughout.

$20+

Sold in 1930

Waffle Iron Catalog Illustrations

L. & H. WAFFLE IRON COLONIAL SQUARE TYPE

Body and base is made of brass, nickel plated. Die cast aluminum grids. Square ebonized handles. Grid size is $6^{1/2}$ x $6^{1/2}$ inches and tray size is 9 x 9 inches. Equipped with a 6ft. silk heater cord, 660 watts.

$25+

Sold in 1928

UNIVERSAL DELUXE STANDARD

Equipped with a 6ft. art silk heater cord and push button switch. Diameter of grids is $7^{1/2}$ inches, diameter of tray is $9^{1/4}$ inches, 660 watts.

Sold in 1928 **$25+**

THERMAX WAFFLE IRON

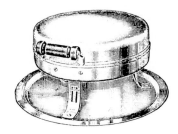

Nickel plated, pure aluminum grids, ebonized handle. Expansion hinge allows clearance for batter to raise. Circular tray attached to the body by perforated air cooled supports. Diameter of grids is $7^{1/2}$ inches. Equipped with a 6ft. heater cord, 660 watts.

Sold in 1928 **$25+**

UNIVERSAL OBLONG WAFFLE IRON

This iron requires no greasing. Permanently attached tray, satin finish center, polished rim. Size of waffles are $3^{1/2}$ x 7 inches. Size of tray is $7^{5/8}$ x $11^{7/8}$ inches. Equipped with a 6ft. art silk heater cord, 650 watts. **$35+**

Sold in 1928

UNIVERSAL DELUXE FANCY

Equipped with a 6ft. art silk heater cord and push button switch. Diameter of grids is $7^{1/2}$ inches, diameter of tray is $9^{1/4}$ inches, 660 watts.

Sold in 1928

$30+

Waffle Iron Catalog Illustrations

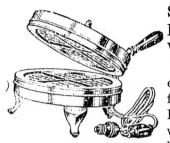

SANITARY ELECTRIC WAFFLE IRON

This waffle iron has several features not usually found on other irons. Plates easily remove for washing without danger to heating parts. Complete with a 6ft. cord, 5½ high, 8 inches diameter.

Sold in 1928

$25+

UNIVERSAL WAFFLE IRON

Solid aluminum, highly polished, ebonized handle and feet, with a separate oval aluminum tray and a switch in cord. Complete with 6ft. art silk cord and separable attachment plug.

$35+   *Sold in 1922*

WAFFLE IRON

Round electric, colonial design, nickel plated iron. 10 inch round tray attached, 7 inch cast aluminum grids. The deep aluminum grid produces a nice thick waffle done to a turn.

$35+

Sold in 1925

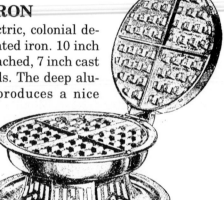

THERMAX WAFFLE IRON

This iron has nickel plated legs, aluminum grid and requires no greasing. The baking is done without smoke or odor. Kromore wire heating element, satin finish frame and a 6ft. cord and separable attachment plug.

$35+

Sold in 1926

HOTPOINT WAFFLE IRON

This iron has nickel plated pedestal base with pierced cool handles. Aluminum plates with cast-in helical core, sheath wire units.
Hinge allows separating of plates for easy cleaning, also permits top plate to rise as waffle cooks.   **$30+**   *Sold in 1926*

BERSTED WAFFLE IRON

Round electric waffle iron 110 volts, nickel plated, 7¼ inch cast aluminum grids, with black ebony handle, and fiber feet and a nichrome heating element in top and bottom molds. Complete with 6ft of super-heater cord equipped with separable attachment plug and detachable contact plug.   **$25+**

Sold in 1927

Waffle Iron Catalog Illustrations

WAFFLE IRON

Round electric waffle iron 110 volts, nickel plated, 8 inch cast aluminum grids, with black ebony handle, and fiber feet and a nichrome heating element in top and bottom molds. Complete with 6ft of super-heater cord equipped with separable attachment plug and detachable contact plug.

Sold in 1927

$20+

HOTPOINT ELECT. WAFFLE IRON

Nickel plated steel body, 7¼ inch aluminum grids, a "Calrod" heating element, expansion hinge, and ebonized handles. Complete with cord and plugs.

Sold in 1928

$35+

BERSTED WAFFLE IRON

A 8 inch aluminum grids, nickel plated body, nichrome heating elements, slotted expansion hinge, groove around edge to catch batter overflow, dull black handles, fiber tipped feet, cord and plug.

Sold in 1928

$25+

UNIVERSAL DE LUXE

Aluminum grids, 7½ inches, nickel plated steel body, expansion hinge, nichrome heating elements, dull black handles, complete with cord and plug.

$25+

Sold in 1928

HOTPOINT WAFFLE IRON

Aluminum grids, 7¼ inches, nickel plated steel body, calrod heating elements, expansion hinge, black enameled wood handle, cord and plug, 12 inch nickel plated tray.

Sold in 1928

$30+

HOTPOINT WAFFLE IRON

Aluminum grids, 7½ inches, nickel plated steel body, calrod heating elements, expansion hinge, dull black handles, cord and plug.

Sold in 1928

$35+

HEET DELUXE WAFFLE IRON

Shell is made of heavy brass with engraved etching, finished in high polished nickel plate. Ample expansion hinge, drip catcher on edge of plates in addition to a large base which acts as a tray and drip catcher.

Sold in 1928

$25+

MARION WAFFLE IRON

Hand-laced elements, polished nickeled finish, pure aluminum griddles, 8 inches, ebonized octagonal wood handles. Complete with 6ft of cord and two-piece attachment plug.

$35+

Sold in 1929

Waffle Iron Catalog Illustrations

WAFFLE IRON

Nickel plated, 7¼ inch base, 9½ inch plate. Plate is made of solid aluminum, highly polished, shaped for conveniently catching overflowing batter. This iron matches the Louis XIV Urn and Percolator. **$35+**

Sold in 1928

HOMELECTRIC WAFFLE IRON

Nickel plated on brass, this 7½ inch aluminum grids, insulated tray attached. Must be greased first time used.

Sold in 1928 **$20+**

OLD ENGLISH PATTERN WAFFLE IRON

Chromium plate, blue diamond finish, ivory antique casein handles and feet. Push button switch attachment plug. Aluminum grids, 7½ inches in diameter. **$35+** *Sold in 1929*

CHINA TOP WAFFLE IRON

Heat gauge that shows when the iron is hot enough to pour in batter, large diecast aluminum grids, patented expansion hinge, guaranteed heating element, drip-proof ring, sparkling chrome finish. **$70+**

Sold in 1928

HOTPOINT TRINITY WAFFLE IRON

This iron has correct baking temperature for making perfect waffles automatically maintained at all times, it never gets too hot nor too cold. Equipped with reliable heat indicator that tells when to pour batter, also the current does not have to be turned off as waffle iron is in use. A polished nickel finish, smooth 7¼ inch die cast aluminum grids, complete with an expanding hinge, and an air cooled base.

Sold in 1931

$35+

"LOW BOY" WAFFLE IRON

Finished in chromium plating – will not rust, stain or tarnish. Heat indicator tells you when to pour batter. Spider heating unit insures even distribution of heat which makes for better waffles. Die cast aluminum grids, bakelite attachment parts and plug with a patented expansion hinge.

Sold in 1931

$25+

Waffle Iron Catalog Illustrations

No. 563C1540 – 1931-32 BLUE LINE AUTOMATIC WAFFLE IRON

This waffle iron never gets too hot nor too cold. A red light burns until time to pour batter, when the batter is poured light appears again. Then set the lever for any degree of brownness you desire. When red light goes out you have just the kind of waffles you want, the same every time. This sparkling chromium finished waffle iron has a timing lever, die cast aluminum grids, air cooled base, genuine bakelite handles, spider heating element, with expansion hinge.

$40+　　*Sold in 1931*

Sold in 1931

No. 563C982 – SUPER BLUE LINE AUTOMATIC WAFFLE IRON

This modernistic designed waffle iron, makes perfect waffles every time. When the iron is ready for baking, a light in the base flashes on, pour in the batter and the light goes out, then set the time lever for the degree of brownness you like. When the light appears again you will have waffles just the way you like them. The current shuts off when waffle is done. Octagon 8inch grids with drip catcher require greasing only the first time.

$70+

No. 563C898 – WAFFLE IRON

A highly polished nickel-plated finish, colored handles and cord. Cast aluminum, 7 inch grids require greasing only first time. Nichrome ribbon with mica heating elements.

$25+

Sold in 1931

No. 40– HOMELECTRIC WAFFLE IRON

Aluminum grids are 7½ iches. Insulated tray attached, beautifully nickel plated.

$25+

Sold in 1931

Waffle Iron Catalog Illustrations

SPECIAL WAFFLETTE IRON

Highly polished nickel plated waffle iron with $7\frac{7}{8}$ inch diameter with aluminum grids $5\frac{1}{2}$ inch in diameter. Fitted with hooded, hinged top and finished in a highly polished nickel plate.

$25+

Sold in 1932

WAFFLETTE IRON

The wafflette iron is for smaller size waffles. Equipped with a 6 inch silver finish, die cast, aluminum grids that make full plate size waffles. This design is of the highly favored plain Colonial pattern with front lift handle. The element is made of nichrome wire to assure ample heat and has a 6ft. silk cord with bakelite contact plug.

$25+

Sold in 1932

TORRID INDICATOR WAFFLE IRON

Equipped with an indicator which insures just the right temperature. No mistakes in starting to bake before the iron is hot enough. A copper shell chromium plated to a mirror-like finish and Kaylith handles.

Sold in 1932 **$40+**

CASSEROLE TYPE COLONIAL WAFFLE IRON

It is chromium plated and fashioned in the plain Colonial style. The indicator is placed on top for convenient reading which is an aid to the operator in baking waffles. Silver finish grids 8 inches across and is fitted with drip ring, also a closed expansion hinge, with bakelite handles and lift. Nichrome wire element assures heat. Included is a silk black cord with white tracer, bakelite contact and one-half attachment plugs.

$25+

Sold in 1932

Waffle Iron Catalog Illustrations

CASEROLE TYPE SEA WAVE TOP WAFFLE IRON

Sold in 1932

Casserole shape, lowboy model, sea-wave top, with indicator, chromium plated finish, bakelite top lifter and side handles, footed base.

$50+

THOMAS A. EDISON EDICRAFT WAFFLE BAKER

Sold in 1933

An automatic waffle baker that makes three large diamond shaped waffles and can be used for baking cakes or cookies. Steel construction with die cast aluminum grids, bakelite feet and handles.

$80+

CHINA TOP WAFFLE IRON

Sold in 1933

Lowboy design with an inlaid top of heat proof china, hand decorated with floral design. Heat indicator in center tells you when to pour batter. Bakelite handles, sturdy construction, die cast aluminum grids.

$70+

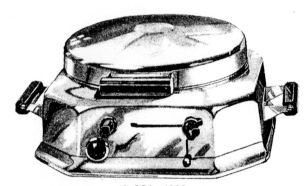

Sold in 1933   **$35+**

WAFFLE-MASTER

Makes waffles with no mess, no need to watch over them, no burning, no smoking and no sticking.

UNIVERSAL WAFFLE IRON, HAMILTON PATTERN

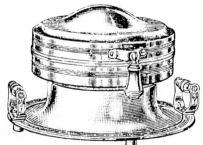

Chromium plated, highly polished, ivoroy casein handles, knobs and feet. Pure aluminum grids that are 7½" in diameter.

$25+   *Sold in 1934*

The expansion hinges permit the cover to rise as the waffle bakes, the heat indicator tells when grids are at correct baking temperature. Complete with 6ft of art silk cord and plugs.

SUNBEAM WAFFLEWITCH

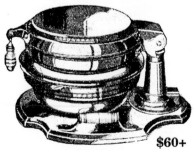

Grids swing aside and the batter bowl and ladle are uncovered. One ladle of batter makes one perfect waffle. When the heat indicator says "hot",

$60+   *Sold in 1934*

pour in the batter, then swing the grids back into place, covering the batter and ladle complete. Chromium plated, ivory finish handles.

Waffle Iron Catalog Illustrations

STREAMLINE WAFFLE MAKER DE LUXE

Fully chromium plated with black handles and knobs and feet. With a heat indicator which shows when waffle maker is ready for the batter. Complete with 7½ inch aluminum waffle grids.

Sold in 1938   **$40+**

TOASTMASTER WAFFLE-BAKER

Fully automatic, the red light glows when the waffle is browned to perfection. Finished in chromium and black.

$25+   *Sold in 1938*

Sold in 1938   **$90+**

TWINOVER WAFFLE IRON

Bakes two waffles at the same time, evenly and perfectly. Deep, clean cut grids and special nichrome heat elements, and a bake indicator on the top to tell you when the iron is hot enough to bake. Finished in chromium and rich walnut bakelite mounts.

Sold in 1938

$90+

"TWINOVER"

This automatic waffle baker does everything but mix the batter and pour it in. Has an overflow batter troughs in addition to all the other "twinover" features.

PURITAN WAFFLE IRON

This Manning-Bowman single type waffle iron has all the automatic features of a "Twinover". The red light tells you when the waffle is done to your liking. Finished in chromium with walnut trimmings, and a batter trough to catch any surplus batter.

$25+

Sold in 1938

Waffle Iron Catalog Illustrations

UNIVERSAL TWIN WAFFLE

Chromium plated, highly polished, solid walnut handle and feet, pure aluminum grids, with expansion hinges to permit the cover to rise as waffles bake. Complete with 6ft. of art silk cord and plugs.

Sold in 1938

$30+

WAFFLE IRON

Modern designed iron in lustrous chromium plated finish with black trim. Equipped with three

Sold in 1939

$20+

heat indicator, 7" aluminum grids and a deep batter trough to catch overflows.

WAFFLE IRON

Adjustable heat regulator for light, medium or crisp waffles. Automatic signal light indicator tells you when

Sold in 1939

the grids are ready to take the batter and again when the waffles are done. Finished in durable chromium, ebony inlay, and ever-cool bakelite handles.

$40+

WAFFLE-BAKER

Toastwell waffle baker is fully automatic and equipped with a special thermostatic control for light or dark

$35+

Sold in 1939

waffles. The ruby jewel pilot light glows until the waffle is browned to perfection, then automatically goes out. Equipped with 8" cast aluminum grids and an extra outer ring which prevents overflow of batter.

DEVONSHIRE PATTERN COMBINATION WAFFLE IRON & SANDWICH TOASTER

Has a nichrome wire wound on thick mica core that assures fast and even toasting. Waffle grids bakes all kinds of waffles and has a drip cup for excess grease. Mahogany composition trim, chromium plated. This can also be used to toast sandwiches, fry eggs, chops, bacon or small steaks. Top grid turns back for making four pancakes at a time.

$40+

Sold in 1940

FOSTORIA WAFFLE IRON with LADLE

This brilliantly polished all-chrome finished waffle iron has die-cast aluminum grids, a dependable heat indicator, double heating elements in base and cover, and walnut bakelite handles.

Sold in 1940

$40+

Waffle Irons

VICTORY BRAND MINIATURE WAFFLE MAKER

Type AFU, nickel plated iron with wood handle, 300 watts, 5" diameter. By Chicago Electric Manufacturing Co., Chicago, IL.
$20+

1940 UNIVERSAL WAFFLE IRON

Model EA-3001, chrome with brown bakelite handle, 110 volts, 660 watts. This wheat pattern came with matching toasters (pop up & clam shell), coffee maker, and rectangular waffle iron. By Landers, Frary & Clark, New Britain, Conn.
$40+

1934 MANNING-BOWMAN

Chrome waffle iron with black bakelite and wood handles, 11" dia. x 4½" tall, 110-120 volts, 800 watts. By Manning Bowman & Co., Meriden, Conn.
$20+

LANDERS WAFFLE IRON

No. E5334N chrome with black bakelite handles, 9¾" dia. x 4¾" tall, 108-116 volts, 660 watts. By Landers, Frary & Clark.
$35+

Waffle Irons

WESTINGHOUSE "AUTOMATIC" WAFFLE IRON

Chrome waffle iron with porcelain base and black bakelite handles, 11" dia. x 4½" tall, 115 volts, 800 watts (AC only). By Westinghouse Electric & Mfg. Co., Mansfield Works, Mansfield, Ohio, U.S.A.

$75+

THERMAX WAFFLE IRON

No. 1650, chrome with black bakelite handles, 108-116 volts, 660 watts, pat. Nov. 18, 1924, 11" dia. x 5" tall (with handles). By Landers, Frary & Clark, New Britain, Conn., U.S.A.

$20+

UNIVERSAL WAFFLE IRON

No. E7234, chrome with ivory handles, 10" dia. x 7" tall, 108-116 volts, 660 watts. By Landers, Frary & Clark, New Britain, Conn., U.S.A.

$30+

MANNING BOWMAN WAFFLE IRON

Chrome with black bakelite handles, 10" dia. x 6" tall, 106-115 volts, 660 watts. By Manning Bowman & Co., Meriden, Conn., Made in U.S.A.

$30+

Waffle Irons

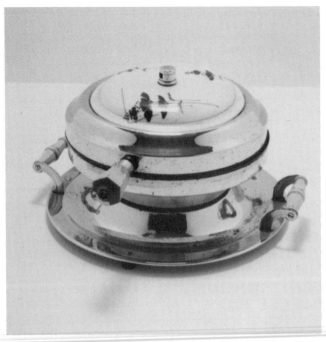

UNIVERSAL WAFFLE IRON
No. 7424B, chrome with red jewel light and black bakelite handles, 110-120 volts, 660 watts, 4¾" tall x 10⅞" dia. Patented Nov. 18-24, by Landers, Frary & Clark, New Britain, Conn. U.S.A.

$25+

ROYAL ROCHESTER WAFFLE IRON
Model 12840, chrome with a painted porcelain top and wood handles, base 10" dia. x 6" tall, 110-120 volts, 660 watts. By Robeson Rochester Corp., Rochester, NY.

$70+

VICTORY BRAND WAFFLE IRON
A Handyhot Product, 105-120 volts, 660 watts, 7" tall x 9" dia. By Chicago Electric Mfg. Co., Chicago, IL.

$20+

ESTATE WAFFLE IRON
No. 75 Porcelain enameled waffle iron with bakelite switch on cord with wooden handles, 110 volts, 5 amps, 9" dia. base x 6½" tall. By The Estate Stove Co., Hamilton, OH.

$50+

Waffle Irons

GENERAL ELECTRIC WAFFLE IRON
Chrome with black bakelite handles, 115 volts, 550 watts, 4" tall x 12" dia. By General Electric Co., Bridgeport, Conn. Ontario, Calif.
$45+

ROYAL ROCHESTER WAFFLE IRON
Type W.A., #E-6472, 108-115 volts, 600 watts, 5" tall x 10" dia. By Robeson Rochester Corp., Rochester, NY.
$30+

BERSTED WAFFLE IRON
Chrome with wood handles, 9½" dia. (no handles), 10½" dia. w/handles x 6¾" tall. By Bersted Mfg. Co., Fostoria, Ohio.
$30+

COLEMAN WAFFLE MAKER
Model 10, chrome with black bakelite handles, 625 watts. By The Coleman Lamp and Stove Company, Wichita, KS.
$65+

Waffle Irons

MANNING-BOWMAN WAFFLE IRON

Chrome iron with ivory handles, 800 watts, advertised in 1946 magazine. By Manning-Bowman, Meriden, Conn.

$40+

1940 TOASTMASTER WAFFLE BAKER

Model 2D2, chrome iron with brown bakelite handles, 120 volts, 5.9 amps. By McGraw Electric Co., Toastmaster Division, Elgin, IL.

$20+

1937 TOASTMASTER WAFFLE BAKER

Model 2D1, chrome with black bakelite handles, 750 watts. By McGraw Electric Co., Minneapolis, MN.

$20+

1935 UNIVERSAL WAFFLE IRON

Chrome iron with black bakelite handles, type E7704, 110 volts, 660 watts. By Landers, Frary & Clark, New Britain, Conn.

$20+

Waffle Irons

1940 WESTINGHOUSE WAFFLE IRON
Chrome with brown bakelite handles, 600 watts. By Westinghouse Electric & Mfg. Co., Mansfield Works, Mansfield, Ohio.
$20+

1940 G.E. WAFFLE IRON
Chrome iron with ivory bakelite handles, 115 volts, 800 watts. By General Electric, Bridgeport, Conn.
$25+

DOMINION WAFFLIE IRON
Style 5145, chrome iron with black bakelite handles, 660 watts, streamlined skirt and handles. By Dominion Electric Mfg. Co., Mansfield, Ohio.
$25+

SENECA WAFFLE IRON
Chrome iron with black bakelite handles, 115 volts, 625 watts. By Seneca Co., Brighton, NY.
$30+

Waffle Irons

RAINBOW WAFFLE IRON
Model 80W, chrome iron with black bakelite handles, 115 volts, 600 watts. By Precision M.F.G., Dover, New Jersey.

$20+

1940 WESTINGHOUSE WAFFLE IRON
Chrome iron with black bakelite handles, 750 watts. (The extra low-slung design calls for a specially designed heating element). By Westinghouse Electric & Mfg., Co., Mansfield, OH.

$25+

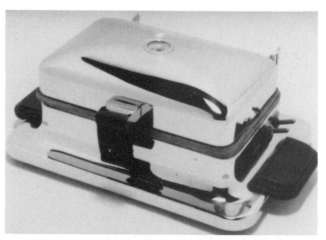

1939 TWIN-O-MATIC WAFFLE IRON
Chrome iron with brown bakelite handles, 1000 watts, a futuristic design, bakes two waffles at once. By Manning-Bowman, Meriden, Conn.

$90+

SEARS ROEBUCK WAFFLE IRON
Model 307-6604, chrome iron with wood handles, 600 watts.

$20+

Waffle Irons

WESTINGHOUSE WAFFLE IRON

Type A, style 234186, pat. April 20, 1909, 9¾" x 8¾" x 5¾". By Westinghouse E & M Co., Mansfield Works, Mansfield, Ohio. **$35+**

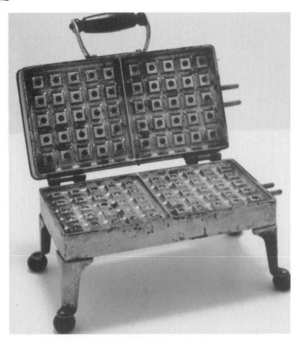

THERMAX WAFFLE IRON

No. E3931, aluminum with wood handles, 115-120 volts, 5.1 amps, 8½" x 5" x 4¼". By Landers, Frary & Clark, New Britain, Conn. U.S.A. **$35+**

MADE-RITE WAFFLE IRON

Model 2221, chrome iron with wood handles, 600 watts. By Made-Rite Corp., Mansfield, OH. **$30+**

1937 K-M ELECTRIC TWIN WAFFLE IRON

Chrome with black bakelite handles, 115 volts, 600 watts, 16" x 4½" x 8¼". By Knapp-Monarch Co., St. Louis, MO, U.S.A. **$30+**

KWIKWAY DOUBLE WAFFLE IRON

Chrome with painted wood handles, 600 watts, advertised in 1938. By Kwikway Co., St. Louis, MO. **$35+**

HEATMASTER TWIN WAFFLE IRON

Style 307-366, chrome with wood handles, model 590, 700 watts, 110-120 volts, 15" x 4½" x 9¼". By D.E. M., Inc. **$30+**

The New Hankscraft Fiesta Egg Service Set

HANKSCRAFT *Fiesta* EGG COOKER *and* EGG SERVICE SET

COOKS EGGS JUST THE WAY YOU LIKE THEM--RIGHT AT THE TABLE

The egg cooker boils, scrambles and shirrs eggs quickly and accurately by electricity in live steam. A few teaspoons of water poured into the cooker turn to steam within a few seconds; the amount of water governs cooking time. Current shuts off automatically when eggs are done. Finished in Fiesta Red Porcelain with glistening chrome dome. Complete with boiling tray and poacher.

Item No. 874
(Fiesta Egg Cooker),
Price $6.90

The new brilliantly colorful Fiesta Egg Service Set in Gay Fiesta colors—vivid red, yellow, blue and green—with gleaming chrome and clear maple, brings new charm to your breakfast table. This new set, shown above in actual colors, includes Hankscraft Automatic Electric Egg Cooker (described at left), four vari-colored Fiesta egg cups, ivory poaching dish, Fiesta salt and pepper shakers and maple plywood tray.

Item No. 880 (Fiesta Egg Service),
Price $13.70

Standard Model EGG SERVICE SET

This pleasing ensemble includes the standard automatic electric egg cooker described below, four matched double egg cups, and gleaming chromium plated serving tray. Choice of green, blue or ivory.

Item No. 8151 (Standard Egg Service),
Price $9.90

Standard EGG COOKER

Four egg capacity automatic electric egg cooker complete with boiling tray and egg poacher. Eggs boiled or poached in this modern manner taste better and are more nutritious because of the gentle cooking action of live steam. Finished in green, blue or ivory with chrome plated dome.

Item No. 815 (Standard Egg Cooker), Price $5.60

Special Model EGG SERVICE SET

Includes special cooker (described below) with four matching egg cups with enameled serving tray. Choice of ivory, green or blue. The season's outstanding electrical gift at a surprisingly low cost.

Item No. 800-B (Special Egg Service), Price $5.60

Special EGG COOKER

A four-egg capacity Hankscraft Automatic Electric Egg Cooker with ivory, green or blue base and top, and flashing chrome dome. Operates exactly like more expensive cookers. Boils eggs in live steam. Starts instantly—shuts off automatically. Amount of water governs cooking time. An outstanding value.

Item No. 794-B (Special Egg Cooker), Price $2.80

Miscellaneous

WARING BLENDOR
Model DL-202, 115 volts, 510 watts. By Winsted Hardware Mfg. Div., Winsted, Conn.
$25+

1936 WARING BLENDOR
This rocketship designed blendor was named after the famous band leader, Fred Waring, 115 volts, 3 amps. By Waring Products Corp., New York, NY.
$60+

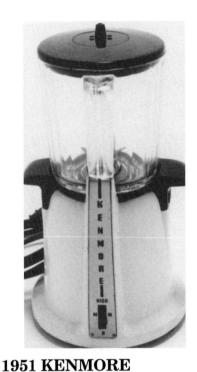

1951 KENMORE BLENDOR
Model 116-82421, two speed, small mixing glass, top has small access hole for adding ingredients while mixing, 120 volts, 250 watts, 2.5 amps.
$55+

 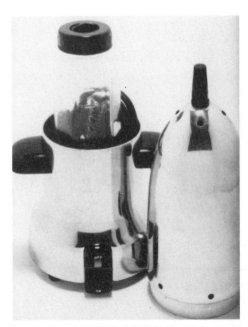

1956 SUNBEAM AUTOMATIC BABY BOTTLE WARMER
Model B2, aluminum with black bakelite, Rocketship design is rare. By Sunbeam Corp.
$75+

Miscellaneous

1943 SUNBEAM AUTOMATIC EGG COOKER

Model E, A.C. only, with original cardboard insert and tag, 5¼" dia. (no handles), 6½" tall. By Sunbeam Co.

$25+

HANKSCRAFT EGG COOKER

No. 815, porcelain and chrome, pat. 1943, 115 volts, 3 amps, base is 4½" dia. x 5¾" tall. By Hankscraft Company, Madison, WI.

$45+

1954 SUNBEAM EGG COOKER

Model E2, aluminum with bakelite handles and feet, base is 4⅝" dia. x 7¾" tall, 110-120 volts, 500 watts. By Sunbeam Corp., Chicago, U.S.A./Toronto, Canada.

$25+

HANDYHOT DEEP FRYER

Aluminum with plastic handles, 110-120 volts, 75 watts, 9¼" diameter x 8½". By Chicago Electric Mfg. Co.

$25+

Miscellaneous

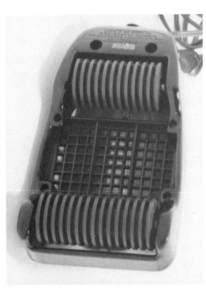

PEKINESE EXTENSION CORD
Porcelain, 31/2" tall x 21/4" wide base.
$60+

ROLL-A-RAY
Model RAR-1, bakelite, 115 volts (AC/DC), 60 watts. Believed to be a roller/massager. Has a hidden 60 watt light bulb to produce gentle heat to massaged area. By O.A. Sutton Corporation, Wichita, Kansas.
$25+

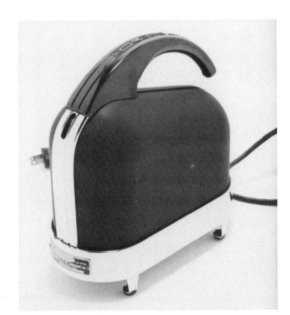

DIFUSOLIER VAPORIZER
Model C, chrome with black bakelite handle, 450 watts. By Tanglefoot Company, Grand Rapids, MI.
$45+

MASSAGING PIN
Patented Jan. 12, 1932, with green bakelite handle, 19³/4" long x 2¹/4" dia.
$30+

CLICK A SWITCH . . .
and a POLAR CUB goes to work

In many thousand homes these nimble aides speed up household routine. Polar Cubs are Christmas gifts that *do things!* Electrical devices built to lift the more tedious little chores right out of housework.

Click the switch of the new all-purpose Polar Cub Beater, and it mixes light batters and mayonnaise, whips cream, beats eggs, to a fluffy lightness, in jigtime.

When you want fresh orange, lemon or grapefruit juice, the Sunkist Junior Juice Extractor swiftly yields every drop without a bit of muss or labor. Mix drinks, salad dressings and other light mixtures with the Polar Cub Mixer, which also whips cream and eggs. Indoor drying, whether hair, lace, wet shoes or clothing, is the job for the Polar Cub Dryer. These are only a few of the modern Polar Cubs.

The heart of every Polar Cub is the triple-tested Polar Cub electric motor, fully guaranteed by its makers.

Look them over on this page. Aren't there *ideal* gifts here for certain people on that Christmas list? Write their names on the margin of the page. Use it as a shopping guide. You'll find Polar Cubs at any modern store. If not, you may mail your order on the coupon, to The A. C. Gilbert Company, 138 Erector Square, New Haven, Connecticut. Or send for Free Booklet.

$11.95
POLAR CUB BEATER
Made Expressly for
THE WESSON OIL-SNOWDRIFT PEOPLE

Mixes mayonnaise and all light batters. Whips cream, beats eggs. It does the job thoroughly and quickly. Its powerful motor and double intertwining agitator aerates evenly. Its standard rod is *curved* to enable the use of large mixing bowls. The blades are easily detached for washing.

• • •

SUNKIST JUNIOR JUICE EXTRACTOR
Adopted by the
CALIFORNIA FRUIT GROWERS EXCHANGE

It provides fresh orange, lemon or grapefruit juice as quickly and easily as turning on a faucet. Press the fruit gently down at the top, and *every drop* of juice gushes from spout. Easy to clean.

$4.95
and
$7.50
for larger size

POLAR CUB MIXER. Just the thing for malted milk, chocolate and other drinks and light mixtures with soda fountain speed and efficiency.

$14.95

$4.95

POLAR CUB HAIR DRYER. There are many uses for it about the house, including drying hair, wet shoes, clothing, laces, etc. It blows a warm, dry current of air.

December 1929 Good Housekeeping

★ **Polar Cubs**

>»>« «·>»>«·>»>« «·>»>« «·>»>« «·>»>« «·>»>«

The A. C. Gilbert Company, 138 Erector Square, New Haven, Conn.

.................Send me "The Book of Polar Cubs—Electrical Helpers for Every Household."

.............My dealer cannot supply me with Polar Cubs.

Send me ....

....

I Enclose $ ....

Name...

Address..

MANNING BOWMAN MEANS BEST

Craftsmen in metal Since 1864

The Manning-Bowman name is a hall mark of supreme quality in electrical accessories; yet the prices here are surprisingly low. An electrical gift is enjoyed all the year round.

Waffle iron

Manning-Bowman quality at low price. Chromium plated waffle iron with heat indicator that takes the guess work out of waffle making. The grids are pure aluminum, 7 inches across; base is 11½ inches wide, with cool ebonized handles. Complete with silk covered cord. Our price leader.

MB3003 Price..... **$8.20**

2-slice automatic toaster

Makes two slices of toast at once, quickly, perfectly, automatically. Toasts both sides of both slices at once, thus sealing all the delicious flavor, delivering it piping hot. Fully automatic—the current snaps off when the toast is ready. An inner crumb drawer catches the crumbs. Finished in brilliant chromium plate, 7½ inches high, base 6x8 inches.

MB3004 Price..... **$19.50**

Complete 9-cup percolator set

Chromium Plated—Gold Lined—Catalin Mounts

New!! Complete 4-piece electric coffee service of highest quality at amazingly low price. The service is beautifully finished in everlasting chromium—it needs no polishing, is always bright and attractive. The percolator urn brews perfect coffee every time, full flavored and clear, by means of an exclusive inner valve syphon. The percolator is protected with a safety fuse device so it can never burn out. Percolator has large 9-cup capacity, is 14 inches high, with beautiful Jade Catalin mounts on side handles, faucet handle and feet. The sugar and creamer are gold lined. The tray is oval shape, 18x12 inches. Complete with silk covered cord; shipping weight, 13 lbs.

MB3001 Complete. Price **$30.70**

AUTOMATIC WAFFLE IRON

Signals with a red light

Bakes waffles to the king's taste, light, medium, or extra crisp. There's no guessing, the waffles are always thick, delicious! A red signal light glows while waffle is baking. The signal light goes out and the current snaps off automatically when waffle is ready. The iron is a new pattern, finished in everlasting bright chromium, with 7 inch pure aluminum grids. A trough catches any overflow batter. The base is 13½ inches wide. Complete with silk covered cord and pull plug, shipping weight 7 lbs. For alternating current only.

MB3002 Price..... **$15.60**

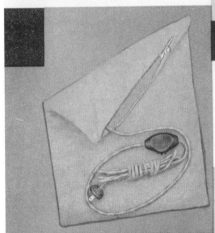

PAD WITH WASHABLE VELOUR COVER

Large heat pad—zipper cover

DeLuxe heating pad with the marvelous new washable velour covering, the most luxurious, downy-soft covering ever made; has zipper top for easy removal. Comes in three lovely pastel colors. The heating unit is highest Manning-Bowman quality, thermostatically controlled, giving three positive heats distributed evenly over the entire pad. No radio interference. The pad is large and flexible, can be wrapped around any part of the body. Its warmth means health and comfort! Size 12x15 inches, comes complete with 10 ft. silk covered cord and pull plug. Shipping weight, 2 lbs. Makes a practical gift—every home should have one.

MB3007 Apple Green. Complete		**$9.40**
MB3008 Orchid. Complete		9.40
MB3009 Peach. Complete		9.40

Handsome M-B 7-cup percolator, chromium on solid copper; safety fuse protected. Brews perfect coffee. Complete with cord and plug.
MB3006 Price..................... **$14.70**

COMBINATION WAFFLE IRON AND GRILL

Bakes—broils—fries—toasts

The perfect table cooker, and a perfect gift! It makes the most delicious toasted sandwiches with the filling inside. You'll use it for grilling steaks, chops, and fish—preparing bacon, eggs, pancakes, hamburgers, etc. Comes with or without waffle grids of pure aluminum size 7x11 inches, for making four waffles at a time. Oversize heating elements in both upper and lower grids! The cooker is finished in everlasting bright chromium, with cool ebonized handles, complete with silk covered cord and double plug.

MB3005 Cooker Only. Price		**$19.50**
MB3010 Complete with Waffle Grids. Price		23.40

The best is always the cheapest

1933

For Reference Only

UNIVERSAL
AUTOMATIC TOASTER

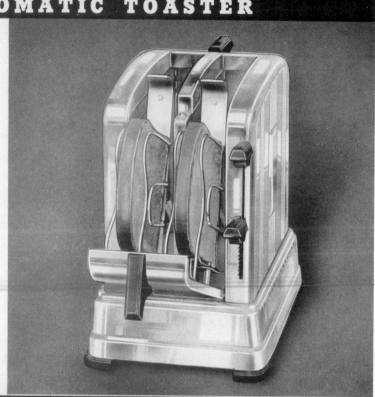

The newest development in Automatic Toasters—always remembers for you—requires no watching and when toast is ready removes it entirely from the oven so there is no chance of it being burned.

It toasts 2 slices of bread at a time .. both sides at once .. size 4 x 4¾ inches .. exactly the way the toast is wanted: light brown, dark brown or medium. Moreover, the toast CANNOT BURN — because this Toaster is equipped with a New Selective Toast-Minder which controls the degree of brownness and removes the toast the moment it is ready! The bread rack automatically tips out and down on hinge. Think of it! Perfect toast every time! Toasted quickly! Toasted easily! No watching necessary.

No. E7822   Each **$17.30**
Full Chromium Plated
Black Bakelite Handles and Feet
Equipped with 6 foot cord

SNACK SET with AUTOMATIC TOASTER

Smart hostesses everywhere welcome this delightful Party Snack Set equipped with the New UNIVERSAL Automatic Toaster—the toaster that requires no watching and leaves the hostess free to devote her attention to her guests. In addition to the toaster, the snack set includes all the other accessories needed to help make parties gay—Walnut Tray size 24½ x 15½ in. made of three-ply walnut which will not warp or stain, and can be easily washed; 5-Compartment Crystal Clear Glass Dish 6¼ x 14¼ in.; Walnut Cutting Block, 4¾ x 14¼ in.; for making sandwiches, Cutting Knife with 7 in. Stainless Steel Blade and Ivory Grained Handle.

No. E87822   Set Complete   Each **$26.70**

BUFFET FOOD SERVER

Everywhere hostesses greet this new electric appliance with enthusiasm. Three heat-resisting removable glass food containers enclosed within the server are heated between 160° and 180° F.—the best temperature no matter how large the party. Late arrivals offer no problem. Ideal for Sunday breakfast or for other meals where schedules are irregular. Capacity of dishes 3 pts. each. Body and Covers Plated with Brilliant Chromium, Solid Walnut Handles and Feet, matching Chevalier Line. Entire Food Server is 19¾ in. long, 10¾ in. wide, 6¼ in. high. Equipped with 6 ft. cord.

No. E7990   Watts 110   Each **$26.70**

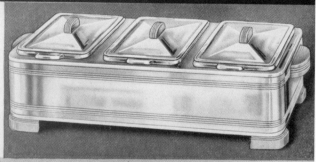

THESE GOODS SOLD ONLY TO MERCHANTS   *Page B*

UNIVERSAL
AUTOMATIC WRINKLE PROOF ROUND HEEL

Only UNIVERSAL has the Wrinkle Proof Round Heel

FINGER-TIP AUTOMATIC CONTROL provides just the right heat for every fabric from dainty silk lingerie to heavy, damp linens. Its Clear-Sight Dial with Black Enamel Inlay Bakelite Indicator adds distinction to this popular model.

WRINKLE-PROOF ROUND HEEL — an exclusive UNIVERSAL feature, has no sharp edges to catch or wrinkle the cloth. It irons backward and sideways as easily as forward.

BEVELED EDGES and TAPERED POINT — slip easily under small or large buttons. Pleats are just no problem at all for this modern SPEED-IRON.

AIR-COOLED BAKELITE HANDLE — UNIVERSAL'S own handfitting, wrist-resting design. Air vents at front and back keep it comfortably cool.

NON-SKID HEEL REST prevents iron from sliding off board and possible accidents.

CHROMIUM FINISH is stain and rust proof. It is hard and highly polished, giving a free easy gliding surface.

Permanently attached 6 ft. cord.

No. E7886   Price $9.20
Weight 6 lbs.   800 watts.

No. E7183   Price $9.20
Weight 3½ lbs.   1000 watts.

UNIVERSAL Electric OVEN ROASTER

Does Everything an Oven will do ROASTS, BAKES and STEWS

CAPACITY — 3 Piece Cooking Set; 5 lb. chicken or 8 lb. rolled beef, 1¼ quarts peas and 8 potatoes. **Aluminum Cooking Well;** 14 lb. ham, 12 lb. turkey or two 5 lb. chickens.

MAGICALLY COOKS LIKE ANY ELECTRIC OVEN AT A VERY SMALL COST

The UNIVERSAL Electric Oven Roaster enables you to enjoy the cool, clean way of cooking with all the speed, economy and certainty of results that electric cookery brings. Meats are roasted with very little shrinkage. Vegetables retain their color and health vitamins. Bread, cakes and biscuits are baked light and fluffy. Cooks dinner for eight.

Requires no watching — no preheating — connects to any wall outlet. Set indicator for temperature desired. Heat is maintained automatically. Asbestos insulation throughout keeps heat in the roaster and much of the cooking is done by stored heat. Light and portable. Gun Metal Exterior. Aluminum cooking well and pans. Chromium Plated Cover.

DIMENSIONS AND CAPACITIES — Height over all 10¾ in., Length 19½ in., Width 13¼ in. **Aluminum Cooking Well** 15½ x 11 x 3⅝ in., capacity 8 quarts. **Aluminum Inset Pans** — One, 11 x 7⅝ x 3⅝ in., with bale handle, capacity 4 quarts. Two, 7½ x 3⅞ x 3⅝ in., equipped with cover and detachable handle, capacity 1¼ quarts each.

No. E9985   Roaster Complete   Each **$26.70**
Complete with 6 ft. Underwriters' Approved Cord.